Surviving
THE ULTIMATE
BETRAYAL

A Woman's Guide to Navigating the
Fallout from Infidelity

Patricia A. Tucker

Copyright © 2018, 2020, 2022 by Patricia A. Tucker

All rights reserved. No part of this book may be reproduced in any form without permission in writing from the author, except for the use of brief quotations in a book review.

Although this publication is created to provide accurate information, neither the publisher nor the author is engaged in rendering professional advice or services to the reader. The ideas, suggestions, and strategies provided in this book are not intended as a substitute for seeking professional guidance. Neither the publisher nor the author shall be held liable or responsible for any loss or damage allegedly arising from any suggestion or information contained in this book.

All Scripture quotations, unless otherwise indicated, are taken from the Holy Bible, New King James Version®. Copyright © 1982 by Thomas Nelson. Used by permission. All rights reserved.

Footnotes taken from *The Nelson Study Bible*, copyright © 1997 by Thomas Nelson. Used by permission of Thomas Nelson. www.thomasnelson.com.

Printed in the United States of America

ISBN 978-0-9997350-0-8

Library of Congress Control Number: 2017919580

Cover design: Kent Locke
Interior design: Rick Soldin

Survivingbetrayal2@gmail.com

To My Parents—None better in the world—I Love You!

Ma—Hugs and kisses, for your charisma, wit, mentoring, support, and your example of a godly woman. I would be remiss if I didn't declare—You are blessed! (Proverbs 31:28)

Pop—Hugs and kisses, for filling up my gas tank, making sure my vehicle was road ready, activating the second phone line so I could get to you and Ma when I needed to. I haven't forgotten.

Thank you both for all of the countless and loving things you've done throughout my life.

Contents

Acknowledgements ix
Fun Fact x
Introduction xi

1 Call It What It Is 1
2 Confession Time 8
3 Where I Went Wrong 13
4 What God Has Joined Together 20
5 Moving Forward 26
6 Too Legit to Quit 32
7 Pray Without Ceasing 37
8 Support Team 44
9 The Other Woman 51
10 Freedom to Forgive 58
11 Surviving 64
12 By Faith 70
13 Fear 78
14 The Children 86
15 Legally Speaking 97
16 A Word of Encouragement 104
17 Life After Divorce 111
18 Don't Hate the Player, Hate the Game 120
19 We're All Human 125
20 And Finally My Sister 132

A Special Gift 134
Notes 136
About the Author 139

Acknowledgements

God, my heavenly Father – for your love and forgiveness, for Who you are, what you have done, and what you will do – for that and so much more, I am tremendously thankful! I'm grateful that you desire to use me and that you didn't give up on me as I was dragging my feet. You are awesome; none can compare to you!!!

My Children – I'm glad God gave me you!! I hold many fond memories of our special moments, including our inside jokes. Thank you for being who you are. Your sense of humor, patience, and your love is unmatched. I couldn't have asked for better children. I Love you!!

My Family – Ma, Pop, Sister, Brother – Thank you for defining what real family is through your undying love, assistance, listening ear, encouragement, and timely wisdom.

Thank you to everyone who played a part in helping this book come to fruition. Every contribution, great and small, is appreciated beyond measure!

Fun Fact

To protect the identity of "the innocent," I thought it would be interesting to use the names of people in the Bible that are also somewhat common today.

Name	Chapter	Reference
Andrew	Throughout the book	Matthew 10:2
Rufus	Call It What It Is	Romans 16:13
Anna	Freedom to Forgive	Luke 2:36
Nicolas	Support Team	Acts 6:5
Lydia	Support Team	Acts 16:14
Julia	Support Team	Romans 16:15
Claudia	Surviving	II Timothy 4:21
Ruth	Surviving	Book of Ruth
Cleophas	Life After Divorce and We're All Human	Luke 24:18 (KJV)

Introduction

Betrayal—who hasn't fallen prey to it?

It infiltrates every status—economic, social, ethnic, financial, and even religious. The betrayal I suffered was infidelity. My experience dealing with the fallout from infidelity began after my husband, Andrew, entered into an adulterous relationship with his old college friend. The affair started before he began pastoring and continued thereafter.

My journey was filled with emotional and situational ups and downs. I loved and truly believed in Andrew. I had always supported him, but to a fault. Although Andrew denied the existence of an adulterous relationship for a long time, I had known the truth about the affair. My internal struggle was undeniably painful, and it was difficult determining where to go, whom to turn to, or what to do. I suddenly found myself navigating roads previously untraveled. In vain I searched for books that could help guide me through the dark and murky roadway of recovery from an affair. I realized that if I suffered for an inordinate length of time, toiling over what to do and how to get through it, then there must be other women who are agonizing over the same dilemmas.

Consequently, God compelled me to write a book birthed from my pain. Ideally, this resource would provide insight, strategies, encouragement, and ultimately hope to women suffering the same fate. I was a pastor's wife; therefore, some sections are specific to that perspective. However, this book is for *every woman* who seeks empowerment by addressing the issues that she may face when her marriage is confronted by adultery. Issues such as fear, legal concerns, and *the other woman*. Prayerfully, the principles learned in this book will help readers successfully navigate and, most importantly, *survive her own personal journey with infidelity*.

1
Call It What It Is

"For every tree is known by its own fruit. For men do not gather figs from thorns, nor do they gather grapes from a bramble bush."
Luke 6:44

"When people show you who they are believe them, *the first time.*" That is wisdom worth heeding, passed on by the late acclaimed poet, Maya Angelou. It is hard to comprehend that someone you love is being unfaithful. But, if that's what they show you, believe it!

If it looks like a duck, acts like a duck and quacks like a duck, the probability is astronomical that it is a duck. If you see indications of infidelity, call it what it is! Nobody wants to think, let alone admit, that their beloved spouse is deceiving them, but it happens. If that is the reality, do not deny it or attach excuses to it. Living in denial will only make matters worse.

Infidelity is a crack in the marital bond. *Merriam-Webster*.com describes it as, having a romantic or sexual relationship with someone other than one's husband or wife. And *Dictionary*.com explains that it is, "a breach of trust or a disloyal act; transgression." This kind of disloyalty reveals itself in varying forms including e-flirting and e-sex (by any electronic means), sex talk, and pornography. Those acts are not small, innocent or harmless. A person who engages in such behavior is in violation of their marital covenant and is treading on treacherous territory. Keeping secrets, defensive behavior, being emotionally (and sexually) distant, and becoming accusatory are some clues that something is going on. Believe your eyes, and your ears!

On occasion, I have seen children misbehaving in public. I've thought to myself, "That's not the first time that child has behaved like that." The child is conceivably acting out at home and getting away with it. Of course, the child didn't just wake up that morning and start trippin'. The same is true with a spouse. It is not likely that he just woke up one morning and started to trip. There were probably overlooked signs along the way. Signs appear for a reason; they serve as warnings. I was given visible signs as far back as when Andrew and I were dating. I *had* the warnings!

We ought to pray about everything. As the Bible instructs, "Be anxious for nothing, but in everything by prayer and supplication, with thanksgiving, let your requests be made known to God" (Philippians 4:6). Unfortunately, I was praying the wrong thing. My prayers were inquiring *if* I should tell. They should have been, "when and to whom." A Christian counseling radio program that I've listened to frequently advised callers to, "do the next right thing." If you know that your spouse is having an affair, what is your next right thing? Through prayer, you can determine what that is.

I was scared to speak up about Andrew's indiscretions, but I should have anyway. James 4:17 says, "…to him who knows to do good and does not do it, to him it is sin." Speaking up is "good" because hubby can be steered back to a right relationship with God as well as get the help needed to correct his behavior. Both actions may, in time, aid in the healing of your marriage. Moreover, keeping it a secret can eventually work against you, as the situation may progressively get worse. Please be aware, while I know this is a

> *If it looks like a duck, acts like a duck and quacks like a duck, the probability is astronomical that it is a duck.*

painful experience, once you have the knowledge, your responsibility shifts. With that in mind, posting information in the church bulletin, the local newspaper, on social media platforms, or standing up during Sunday service to make an announcement is not the recommended path. You may find a little humor in that, but scorned women have chosen vengeful courses of action. There is proper protocol—which I had not contemplated at the time; confiding in the person in authority over your husband and/or ministry is a good place to start. Most pastors have a "covering"—a person to whom they are spiritually accountable. If you do not have a covering or are not married to a pastor, pray and ask God to whom you should go. Because family, friends, and in some cases, the congregation are affected, there is a natural concern about what will happen when the infidelity is exposed. This is why all actions must be done prayerfully, carefully, and without malice.

Andrew knew many pastors and bishops. I had always hoped that at least one of them would perceive his unfaithfulness and address it. That did not happen. Whether we were visiting another church or one was visiting ours, I was hoping they would detect *something*. Clergy are not super human; however, some have discernment i.e. that God given ability to sense things. I was waiting for someone else to speak up, when all along, it was my responsibility; I *knew* something was going on. Why was I waiting for others to figure out what I already knew?

Since I did not adhere to the unwritten protocol of telling the necessary people, I was a passive accessory to his crime. I do not remember all of the excuses that filled my head. Maybe I thought that by speaking up, I was not trusting God. That philosophy is far from the truth. In addition, let me tell you that neither passivity nor denial are viable options. Both behaviors allow the affair to continue.

Perhaps dealing with your situation has become commonplace for you. It has become *familiar*. Being familiar is simply being "well acquainted with something" (*Merriam-Webster.com*). Are you bound in a certain place, emotionally and/or physically because that place has become familiar? On an episode of a TV sitcom, a primary character made a statement synonymous to, "Some people stay in hell because they know the names of the streets." Whoa! That is deep! Does that hold true for you? Are you so well acquainted with your situation and all the mess and drama that comprises your inferno, that you have actually become, dare I say it, comfortable there because you know the names of the streets?

A pastor who is living a *lifestyle* of sin should resign or be relieved of his pastoral duties. He should not minister on any level until he goes through his own process of restoration. This example comes to mind. I was always blessed by the preaching of Pastor Rufus and appreciated his humorous manner of sermon delivery and overall ministry to the church at large. Unfortunately, this megachurch senior pastor became caught up in an adulterous affair. In taking responsibility for his moral indiscretion, he resigned his leadership position. As part of his recovery and return to wholeness, he was accountable to a team of clergy who guided him through the process. When the team prayerfully deemed it appropriate, the ministerial credentials of Pastor Rufus were restored. Not only that, his marriage was restored as well. Yay for Pastor Rufus! He is a great example of restorative hope for leaders who have fallen in sin.

Consistent, willful sinning is a result of broken relationship with God. If your husband is reluctant to admit his sin to his spiritual covering, it can be for a couple of reasons. Maybe it's because of shame, but an even greater probability is that he really is not repentant and is complacent with that broken relationship. Translation: when the opportunity presents itself or he creates the opportunity, he is going to engage in more of the same behavior. True repentance requires action on the part of the violator. He would need to admit his problem and commit to change by word and deed, as Pastor Rufus did.

Sinful behavior should not be overlooked, nor should the pastor be passed along, or "called" to another church. If the sin is not addressed, it will surface and become destructive. Nobody is perfect, including me. However, when a person has the awesome task of ministering to God's people, he (or she) should be in right relationship with God. Being in that right relationship is important and beneficial to the pastor as well as to the congregation.

Additionally, even in this day of "anything goes," the exposure of a pastor living in sin is devastating to a congregation, and they too need to go through a healing process. As with a victimized spouse, the congregation needs to learn how to forgive and trust again. The overseer can help in these areas as well.

If a husband knows that his wife will be silently faithful and committed to him as a good Christian wife, he can count on that and has it in his favor. How long are you willing to drag around the weight of the problem? Does it have you bent over like the Hunchback of Notre Dame? I learned the hard way that you get what you tolerate; people will only do to you what you allow. Do not accept behavior that you do not want. What are you tolerating?

For some people, the way to deal with issues is to avoid addressing them. But of course, that is not dealing with them at all. I am guilty of avoidance. My way of dealing with my circumstances, I am embarrassed to say, was to become a consultant of products demonstrated at home parties. Don't be shocked; it's true. Well, it wasn't quite that simple. I figured this opportunity, in addition to earning a couple of extra bucks, would get my mind off the situation. However, getting my mind off the situation should not have been my objective. The plastic product party gig *seemed* to present itself at a good time. I was hiding from my reality. I determined that I was not going anywhere. I made a commitment to my husband, and despite it all, I wanted my marriage. My intentions were good, nevertheless, my actions were misguided. I did not respond as I should have. I did not take action.

When I first started seeking counsel because of the affair, I solicited the advice of an older Christian woman who I knew had gone through a similar ordeal. She offered me guidance, perhaps from her experience. I confided in her that I had been looking through Andrew's things for evidence of an affair. She told me not to look, because if I look, I was bound to find something. That is what I was told, but it really didn't stop me for long; the urge was too great. Before I knew it, I took my spy wear out of retirement and I was back on the prowl. If something was there to find, I wanted to find it. Years later I heard a group of professional counselors advise that if you feel you have just cause to look through his things—look; that married couples *should not* have secrets. Now, I am not suggesting that you rifle through your husband's belongings, even though I'm guilty as charged. I will say this, since you are responsible for your actions, make *prayerfully guided* decisions.

While there may have been serious issues in your relationship that steered it toward infidelity, your husband has no legitimate cause for going outside of the marriage. Nevertheless, in an attempt to shift the focus to make you look like the villain, it would not be uncommon for him to try to play the blame game. Your husband may say the marital discord is your fault and may try to find reasons to initiate a verbal altercation, at any time or for any reason, picking at even the very smallest of things. He may also try to minimize what you are feeling. Beware of that strategy; don't buy into it and don't allow it to get to you.

I hope that you will begin to see things as they are. You cannot change your husband but you can change you. Be mindful that bad situations that go unattended will only get worse with time. Deal with things now or pay the price later. It is to your advantage to pray, seek godly counsel, and disclose it to the right person. Taking a stand can be frightening, yet also empowering and liberating. Call it what it is and take charge of yourself and your situation.

2

Confession Time

"Confess your faults one to another, and pray one for another, that ye may be healed."
James 5:16a

I had been waiting for this moment. It was *confession time*. The day that Andrew finally opened up, we were on the telephone. I was at my job and he was at his. For weeks, I had been trying to gently pry the truth out of him, stating my case with compelling evidence. He was feeling the pressure as the evidence was mounting. Then it happened; he said "yes" to my question, verifying that he had been unfaithful.

The moment that my suspicions were confirmed, I became numb from head to toe. By the grace of God, I managed to still tell Andrew that I loved him. I hung up and left my office in one swift motion and retreated to the restroom for a bona fide cry.

I must be candid, one of my first thoughts was to send the children to Grandma's house and spend time by myself. I reconsidered as I recalled having been by myself, night after lonely night. It was my belief that if I had put space between Andrew and myself at that point, the enemy could gain an even larger grip on our marriage. I also realized that since the confession, it was "open season." Andrew was being vocal about his affair, so the time was ripe to get some "honest" answers to my lingering questions.

As we talked during that week, I did not try to make Andrew give me every little detail that happened because I did not want his vivid memory to lead to temptation to go back into sin. Details

Confession Time

would also cause me unnecessary added pain, as it would be more "stuff" to forgive and forget.

Confession time may or may not happen for you. In the event that it does, be "prayed up." In other words, commit that anticipated conversation with your husband to God. Ask Him to let you see what He sees, allow you to be strong, brave and courageous, to speak only the words that need to be said at that time, and to give you the constraint not to kill him. That is a starter list; I am sure you will come up with other areas specific to your situation to pray about.

Confession time is a delicate yet intense moment. I would suggest that you not have this conversation in the kitchen where you have easy access to frying pans, hot grits cooking on the stove, knives or any other weapons of mass destruction! During this time, your response is going to be *your response*. For instance, you might yell, cry, scream and/or throw things (don't throw the good stuff); they are all legitimate reactions. Please have them. Note, however, that at some point your husband will need your ear. When you settle from your initial reaction, you need to be present, so this important conversation can commence. The discussion can be the beginning steps toward healing your marriage, and defeating the devil.

You have been waiting for months and maybe years for this critical moment. Now you are face to face with it. Oh, my! What next? This is one reason why I recommend that you stay prayed up. In doing so, God will order your steps when you don't know what to do. Food for thought—If the tables were turned, how would you want events to transpire?

Although you are genuinely hurting and may want to shut down, keeping the lines of communication open is necessary and may prove to be beneficial. Just imagine what would have happened if the father of the prodigal son turned him away. When the son was still down the road, the father didn't know if he wanted more money, or what condition he was in, nor did he care. Upon seeing his son, the father did not prop himself in the doorframe, tapping his foot with folded arms, waiting to read a list of his son's violations or an estimated calculation of total losses. Instead, he positioned himself for reconciliation, even though he may have been oblivious about what his son actually wanted or did. The father just knew that his son was on his way home, and *that* was cause for celebration. If the father turned the son away, there would have been no reconciliation.

To be positioned for reconciliation you must begin with the proper mindset. If the mindset is right, the appropriate behavior should follow suit. Also, what comes out of your mouth and the actions displayed have to be on one accord. If your mouth is saying, "I'm here for you. I want to help," your body language must not be saying, "I don't care if you find the tallest building and jump! As a matter of fact, I'll push you! Wait one minute, let me get my keys and I'll drive you there!" I know that is a lot for body language to declare, but some of us can pull it off. As I examined the response of the father to his returning prodigal son (Luke 15:20), I concluded that the mindset should be open, welcoming, forgiving, compassionate, and accepting—not of his behavior, but of him. While the relationship and scenario is different, the message is comparable. It is a characterization of us as sinners going back to our forgiving Father. It is also a model of how to forgive in relationships.

> *To be positioned for reconciliation you must begin with the proper m indset.*

Love is powerful. Love is what led God to send Jesus to die for our sins. Letting your husband know every day, in some way, that you still love him can be an important component to the restorative process. To invite healing as the days go by, it would be wise not to throw little "salty" remarks into his wound. I am sure that you can think of many things that you *could* say. If his confession is sincere, believe it or not, he is hurting too. By throwing salt into the wound, you may only exacerbate the pain and prevent the confession from turning into repentance.

If you *can* speak—you may not want to or be able to say anything—speak words of life to him straight from the Word of God as well as the affirmations that you know will build up your man. Some things you say I am sure will be by faith, because you do not see it or you do not feel it. That is okay, speak it by faith.

The healing process takes time for both parties. It's not just all about his needs. Beware that your husband may try to minimize or even dismiss your feelings, especially if he thinks that you are taking too long to get through it. If he really wants to work on the relationship, he should allow *you* the space and time you need to heal and not expect it to happen in *his* time. Communicate to him what you need him to do to help you through the process plus what changes you need to see in him. You are entitled to your feelings and to process through a grieving period. The key word is *through*. It is unhealthy to take up permanent residency in a "state" of grieving. Allow professional Christian counseling, along with the love and support of trusted friends and family to assist you through this ordeal. (Please refer to *Support Team* chapter.)

Getting back into the flow of everyday life can be challenging. The first time that we were intimate after he confessed to me, was very difficult emotionally. I can remember stopping in the moment, getting up and running to the shower, where I cried profusely. All of a sudden I could feel the pain of the past and the uncertainty of the future crashing. It was an agonizing time! I needed to learn how to be patient with the process of healing and I recommend the same for you.

Sincere confession and repentance gives a couple an opportunity for a fresh start. During this time, live in the present, one day at a time, not in the future of the "what ifs." Time in and of itself does not heal wounds, as the saying suggests. It takes God, prayer, individual growth, effort, and commitment *in* time to heal the wounds.

3
Where I Went Wrong

> "Moreover if your brother sins against you, go and tell him his fault between you and him alone. If he hears you, you have gained your brother. But if he will not hear, take with you one or two more, that 'by the mouth of two or three witnesses every word may be established.'"
> Matthew 18:15-16

It's great when confession time takes place and then real change occurs. However, it doesn't happen for everyone. Too bad I can't say, "…and we lived happily ever after." True, my husband confessed infidelity to me. He said that he would stop and I believe that he did…temporarily. But he returned to it. *Why?* I will get to that in a minute, but first I need to admit something. It is hard to share the information in this chapter, because I am embarrassed and ashamed of my tolerance of the affair and Andrew's behavior. However, I know that my candidness will help someone else who is struggling in a similar situation.

To analyze where I went wrong in thorough detail, I really could start with the warning signs displayed even before we were married. However, I will start with some warning signs exhibited after marriage…

- ~ Pager messages that ended with 5-4-7-7 (KISS)
- ~ E-mails / e-cards to and from the other woman
- ~ Condoms in his workout bag (*we* didn't use condoms)
- ~ Cell phone bills documenting numerous calls to and from the other woman

Yes, a pager. I know that dates me. I did not see all of the signs at once; some were revealed in phases before Andrew confessed and some after. Sadly, it was a couple of years later by the time Andrew finally owned up to his involvement with "the other woman."

While I cannot take responsibility for Andrew's actions, there are things I should have done to try to prevent his return to the affair. My passive-aggressive, non-confrontational disposition caused me to not deal with the situation in the manner that it should have been handled. Consequently, since I didn't deal with it, it dealt with me! Passive behavior will only enable your husband to do what he wants. The opposite of passive is "active" and "assertive." For change to take place, something must be done—an active, assertive approach!

When I first had enough tangible evidence of an affair, I should have taken several steps to assist Andrew and me in getting help. As I was praying throughout the entire ordeal, I should have confronted my husband, informed our bishop, and connected with a spiritually based support team.

Action	Rationale
Pray	It is always important to communicate with God for direction, discernment and wisdom, receive comfort, and unload the burden. Make sure to openly and actively listen and watch for His response(s), both typical and atypical.
Confront Spouse	Approach your husband with the information / evidence that you have.
Tell Spiritual "Covering"	Most pastors have someone who is in authority over them in ministry—tell that person. He or she can monitor your spouse, hold him accountable, and can relieve him of his pastoral duties as seen fit. He/she may also assign an accountability partner, peer, or mentor to him. *
Support Team	A spiritually based team can render needed support, comfort you with Scripture, and pray for and with you.

If your husband is one in authority as a spiritual leader, the sins he commits affects the lives of many people. Therefore, advising your bishop or spiritual covering of continuing sinful behavior is imperative. *If your husband is not a pastor, you may go to your pastor or the elder/deacon assigned to your family, or to an appropriate leader in your church.

Now, let's take a quick look at why a woman, any woman, might stay in a bad relationship. I believe it could be out of fear of what she would lose i.e. companionship, status, finances, friendships, the ministry, (which can result in lost souls) and of course, her family—an extremely important dynamic. All of these are legitimate concerns, but the possibility of losing these things remain if something is not done. I did not have high status or big money, but I paid a hefty price for not making the right decision—the decision to speak up. I am confident the outcome would have been different in our marriage and with the ministry if I had confided in and shared what was going on with the spiritual leaders who could have helped.

I did hear "warning bells" that challenged me to expose the situation. In retrospect, those "ring-a-ding-dings" could have been God's answer to my prayers. Maybe what caused my internal debate, at least in part, was that I had seen the "stick it out" mentality modeled before me by several women. In my mind, the "till death do us part" principle was in full effect. I was also under the mistaken assumption that if I just fasted and prayed, God would work it out—*God* would do the exposing. I did not think that *I* was supposed to be the source. Furthermore, it was a job that I did not necessarily want. My hope was for at least one of the many clergy that Andrew knew to "discern" what was going on and address it.

I thought that all I had to do was pray it through. Yeah, just pray it through and let God do all the work. I was sadly mistaken!

Once I said, "Amen" and rose from my knees, I should have taken action. Faith without works is "sho'nuff" dead (James 2:14-26)! You can pray until your knees get raw and fast until you become skeletal, but you must actively do something to effect change. A passive approach to change could eventually lead to divorce.

Divorce is not God's will, and I did not believe it to be an option for me. I wanted to stick it out. God's desire is for the husband and wife to work through difficulties and to reconcile and live as one in harmony. Throughout His Word, God gives us the necessary elements to make marriage work. Yet divorce was allowed. "...Moses, because of the hardness of your hearts, permitted you to divorce your wives, but from the beginning it was not so" (Matthew 19:8). Two significant themes of the Bible are forgiveness and reconciliation; we see various illustrations woven throughout its pages. Isn't that what God did for mankind through Jesus Christ (Ephesians 4:32, II Corinthians 5:17-19)? He forgave us and reconciled the broken relationship between Him and us. Even in the face of a tumultuous marriage, forgiveness and reconciliation can still be the goal. It is still attainable.

> You can pray until your knees get raw and fast until you become skeletal, but you must actively do something to effect change.

I did not predetermine how many rounds my bout with Andrew would be, because when we married, I didn't even know that I would have to step into the ring. I ended up staying in the ring much longer than I should have, fighting with my eyes closed. Be aware of what is going on in your life. You determine your limits, without allowing yourself to be abused. Every individual's situation is exactly that, individual. Each person has to make decisions that are appropriate for her own circumstances. Make your decisions prayerfully and follow through with action.

Decision-making and forging change is paramount. Change is merely doing things another way. If there is a desire for different results, things must be done differently. Step back and evaluate,

Where I Went Wrong

then you will be able to approach the circumstance from an alternate angle. Sometimes implementing change is painful, but the pain of change is better than the pain of staying in the current situation. A marriage plagued by adultery is on sinking sand. Without a doubt, changes are needed. Therefore, with absolute determination, choose a different method.

After dealing with this adulterous situation for a lengthy time, it had taken its toll on me. I started to feel defeated and extremely tired of *everything,* so I began to shut down. Andrew could see how weary I was becoming, so one month we went away for a weekend to talk and try to iron out the most important of our issues—his infidelity. The getaway was strictly for talking—no sex. Our marriage was suffering and the ministry was as well. This could have been a turning point for us, and for the ministry too. I really feel in my heart that at this juncture, God still would have salvaged both. We *verbally* mapped out a plan for Andrew to follow when we returned. The strategy included him eliminating all contact with the other woman—good. But what the blueprint did not include was telling our bishop—not good. I brought the idea up, but Andrew shot it down. One theory on why he did not take my suggestion is that he had no intention of changing. I don't know that to be a fact, it's just a theory—and one in hindsight. By not telling Bishop, Andrew did not receive the reprimand and correction warranted or the accountability factor that he needed. Yes, that is something I ought to have figured out too. I should have insisted that we tell Bishop together, and if not, I could have let Andrew know that I would tell Bishop *without* his approval. I'm pointing out my mistakes so that you can learn from them.

Most women are very busy; my life was no exception. Time went by as life happened and I became distracted and caught up in the daily grind. I fell asleep at the proverbial wheel. It is so important to pay attention, but I did not and it cost me dearly. The plan that we set when we went away became a faded memory. It would have been more effective to have had a written, detailed strategy—something concrete and measurable, including a timeline, and then followed it. The timeline would have kept me on track for reaching my desired goal and I would have less likely become derailed by the regular hustle and bustle of life. The vital key to accomplishing the objective was to actually follow the plan. No plan will work without adhering to it.

In order for a marriage to move forward, there must be positive change or the circumstances will at least remain the same, or can get worse. To get started, you can set short and long-term "progress" goals (what you want to accomplish). Using a calendar to mark "goal" dates will help keep you on course. Know that you want to reach a certain point of progress by a particular time. If that does not happen, set a new deadline or go with the next plan. Don't become discouraged if you don't hit your target; keep moving forward. If you find yourself policing your spouse, it is time to refocus. That is not your job. While endeavoring to reach your goals, try being loving and firm, without being overbearing.

I was committed to our relationship and wanted to see the change in Andrew that I had hoped and prayed for. I had a marriage worth fighting for—do you? In fighting for your marriage, you have the right to set boundaries (limits or lines not to be crossed), and to make requirements of him (honesty, faithfulness, open communication, must seek help). You will need to establish consequences if the boundary line is crossed. You also have the right to ask questions and to expect answers. Ask him direct questions and, to help prevent reoccurrences, find out what led to the affair. Some husbands really do want to change, so when you see real effort, acknowledge it, commend him and work with him to foster the change.

I heard a Christian counselor on the radio suggest that a way to know when the affair is over is when you can *see* it and *feel* it, and not just when he *says* it. Plainly put, words are cheap. So what do you sense? His life should be an open book—no secrets and no hidden places. Also, if hubby is really sorry and repentant, he should take the steps necessary to mend your relationship.

Some husbands might think that healing and recovery is a time that can quickly be passed through. It is a process, and just how much time it will take depends on the individuals involved. If you have a trust issue, hubby may need to hear that you are having a problem trusting him and that it may take a while to recover. It is possible to forgive, yet still have issues with trusting your husband. Trust that has been broken needs to be earned back and it needs to be rebuilt. That does not happen overnight.

I expressed the need for change a couple of times in this chapter. Change is crucial to avoid repeating mistakes. Since no one is perfect, each spouse contributes to the breakdown of a marriage. Therefore, change is imperative in the life of *both* spouses. I believe that some reasons why Andrew returned to the affair was because neither of us made any concrete changes. There was no accountability factor from a spiritual overseer, and he did not feel any pressure to stop. Prayerfully make firm changes now that will help prevent regrets later. Putting measures in place and implementing change will keep you from wondering one day where *you* went wrong.

4
What God Has Joined Together

"So then, they are no longer two but one flesh. Therefore what God has joined together, let not man separate."
Matthew 19:6

Many brides and grooms recite similar wedding vows. Promises that require the two consenting adults standing before the preacher, witnesses, and God, to commit to everlasting love and devotion, no matter the situation—good or bad, sick or well, rich or poor. These vows obligate those reciting them to stay the course. This means learning about each other and growing, in addition to pushing through situations, events, and the hard times; just plain old life. Promises, promises, promises! Promises are actually something that God takes very seriously, even if we don't (Ecclesiastes 5:4, 5).

The promises, aka the "covenant vows," are important to God and should be important to a husband and a wife. *Merriam-Webster.com* provides a simple definition of covenant, "a formal and serious agreement or promise." A more adequate explanation of covenant found on biblestudytools.com describes it this way, "The term 'covenant' is of Latin origin (con venire), meaning a coming together. It presupposes two or more parties who come together to make a contract, agreeing on promises, stipulations, privileges, and responsibilities." Of course, in the marital scenario, the covenant should only be between two, a man and a woman, for as long as they both shall live. Statistics attest to the fact that divorce—termination of the covenant—is on the rise.

What God Has Joined Together

Although divorce is prevalent, it does not have to be *your* reality. Unfortunately, my marriage ended in divorce. However, I firmly believe that couples should seek reconciliation. More significantly, I believe that God desires for couples to reconcile and that relationships be restored to the way He ordained the institution of marriage to be. Actually, when God instituted marriage, the plan was for the husband and wife to stay together. The two become one flesh, a permanent fusion. That was God's design from the beginning. Not two become one, and then become two again. It was Moses who "permitted" divorce (Matthew 19:8). However, Jesus amended the divorce ruling by Moses, mandating that divorce be allowed only in the case of sexual immorality (Matthew 19:9). Since that time, man has come up with other reasons or even no reason (no-fault divorce) to sanction divorce.

> *Although divorce is prevalent, it does not have to be your reality.*

Just because you may have a biblical reason to get divorced does not mean that you have to walk through that door. If you are on the fence, prayerfully come to a decision about the future of your marriage. Once the decision is made, you can strategize from there. If you want your marriage, fight for it! Put up your spiritual dukes and fight, making God-directed efforts to reconcile.

Hosea's story is a good example of marital reconciliation when the ultimate betrayal has been committed. The book of Hosea addresses unfaithfulness through the relationship of the prophet Hosea and his adulterous wife Gomer. It is a parallel to Israel's unfaithfulness to God. When I think about Hosea, I almost forget that he was a real man who suffered real pain due to the unfaithfulness of his real wife. As a husband and a father, he too had to pray and work through the challenges that her immoral behavior generated. The Bible does not detail his survival strategies.

However, what is noteworthy is Hosea's obedience to God's voice (Hosea 1:2-3; 3:1-3). God said, and Hosea did, even to the extent of buying back his wife from another man. The story also illustrates faith and trust in God, as well as God's love for His people and Hosea's *love* for his woman.

Traditional wedding vows include the pledge—to *love*. These days, some may wonder what does love have to do with it. That's a concern that begs a response. Love has everything to do with it because, "…*Love* bears all things, believes all things, hopes all things, endures all things" (I Corinthians 13:7). According to I Corinthians 13:8a, love is a *sure* thing. It never fails.

I am not implying that love is all that is needed to restore a broken marriage, but it is an excellent start. If you choose to work on your marriage, begin by managing what you can control. Here are some ideas to get you on your way:

~ Love. It's foundational. I Corinthians 13 gives ingredients on how to love the right way. After being hurt, it may be challenging to love your husband. If the feelings are nowhere to be found, ask God to renew them. Also, I heard, and I concur with, the suggestion to "Begin to *love by faith.*" Faith is what you hold on to until love becomes a reality. Somehow, I believe that there will be daily opportunities to *show* love, in being kind, not puffed up, not rude, not self-centered, and not easily provoked.

~ Make the decision to truly forgive. You can't move forward effectively if you're stuck in unforgiveness. Not forgiving will hold you and your marriage back.

~ Listen to God, as Hosea did. He will direct you. You may not need to buy your husband back in a literal sense but be tuned in to God's voice to learn what He *is* directing you to do.

~ Recognize that the battle is spiritual (II Corinthians 10:3). I mentioned putting up your spiritual dukes. This is why.

What God Has Joined Together

Arm yourself with appropriate weapons to match the battle at hand. Don't bring your flesh to a spiritual fight.

~ Commit your marriage to prayer, even if you don't see anything that looks salvageable. Speak life to it in prayer, aloud, and when talking with others. If you believe your marriage is going to live, don't make "funeral arrangements" by way of negative and destructive talk.

~ Commit to the undertaking. It may be a long haul; stay the course and don't be swayed. Be patient—it's a process.

~ Work on you. Both parties in a marriage must examine themselves to ascertain what part they played in the breakdown of the relationship. It's a good time to ask God to get down all in your nooks and crannies and extract the imperfections. Whatever you see broken that you can fix, actively work on it. Take responsibility, but don't condemn yourself.

Young women of courting age have been told that the way to a man's heart is through his stomach, suggesting that good food will win him over. I'm thinking that scheme has failed many times. I Peter 3:1-4 tells of a more fruitful way for a woman to reach a man.

Wives, likewise, be submissive to your own husbands, that even if some do not obey the word, they, without a word, may be won by the conduct of their wives, when they observe your chaste conduct accompanied by fear. Do not let your adornment be merely outward—arranging the hair, wearing gold, or putting on fine apparel—rather let it be the hidden person of the heart, with the incorruptible beauty of a gentle and quiet spirit, which is very precious in the sight of God.

You reach him through your godly conduct—God's love shining through what you do could win him. It's not through his stomach but through his soul.

Deciding to stay with hubby may bring on opposition from folks who don't understand. Do what you *know* that God is telling you to do. It doesn't matter what others think or how they are viewing your actions. Claim your place next to your husband. That's *your* man.

It is refreshing to hear of couples who have survived infidelity. Some prominent examples are Kobe and Vanessa Bryant, David Letterman and Regina Lasko, and most famously, Bill and Hillary Clinton. Additionally, there are people who divorced and remarried their spouse such as Gavin MacLeod of *Love Boat* fame, Judy Sheindlin aka Judge Judy, and singer Marie Osmond. It is unknown to me, however, why the latter couples split. I wanted to highlight couples that reunited after having been divorced. So, couples do survive infidelity and breakups! Reconciliation, restoration, and reunification are possible.

Unfortunately, there are couples who do not survive the fallout from infidelity. Choosing to divorce is a big decision. It is one of the biggest decisions that a person can make. I understand the desire to end the pain. Nevertheless, divorce should not be the first choice, but carefully and prayerfully considered after attempts to revive the marriage have been exhausted. The high divorce rate would suggest that exhausting attempts is not what is happening.

I know of women who have stated that if their husband cheated on them, they would leave, with no second chance. That is their prerogative, but I feel that goes against the principles of God; it may also go against the marriage vows that they proclaimed. Knowing that your spouse has willfully violated your marriage covenant is very hard and painful to digest. Some don't recover from that life-altering circumstance.

There are various kinds of heart-wrenching betrayals of trust, with betrayal of the marital covenant near the top of that list. Nonetheless, here's the question—"Is *anything* too hard for the Lord?" God asked that of Abraham in the midst of what appeared to Abe to be a problematic situation. Even though my marriage ended in divorce, my answer is emphatically, "*No!* Nothing is too hard for the Lord!" Sometimes people superimpose their helplessness and inabilities on God, thereby minimizing His "ableness." God *is* able—He is able to guide you through a painful divorce. But more importantly, He *is* able to reconcile your marriage.

5
Moving Forward

"...but I press on, that I may lay hold of that for which Christ Jesus has also laid hold of me. Brethren, I do not count myself to have apprehended; but one thing I do, forgetting those things which are behind and reaching forward to those things which are ahead..."

Philippians 3:12-13

Vanessa L. Williams made history in 1983 when she became the first African American chosen to be Miss America. She surrendered her crown the following year after it was revealed that a racy magazine was to publish nude photos she had taken previously. I remember the buzz surrounding the events. The consequences from her young adult decisions were costly—she lost millions of dollars, and great opportunities, along with her pageant title.

However, Vanessa's journey did not end there. She moved forward, and took the entertainment industry by storm. Over her more than thirty-year career, she has garnered several Grammy nominations, numerous awards and an array of film, television, and theater performances. Additionally, she is now an author, and has launched her own clothing line. Amongst all of her many accomplishments, my personal favorite is, lending her voice to the M&M's® character, *Ms. Brown*. One day I will meet her, but from afar, she appears to be the epitome of elegance and grace in spite of all the turmoil she had to endure.

One reason Vanessa L. Williams is my "shero" is because she survived a betrayal of trust and confidentiality that could have permanently destroyed her as a person, as well as any potential for a prosperous career. Now, her success speaks for itself. Vanessa's story is inspirational for anyone striving to move forward while conquering their own setbacks.

Vanessa moved forward; I moved forward. Whether you are still with your husband, separated with hopes of reconciliation, or headed for divorce, *you must move forward*. Moving forward is essential mentally, emotionally, and for some, even physically. What was, isn't anymore. There is a new horizon waiting for you; embrace it. It can be a harsh reality, but life goes on, so go on with your life. You are not alone, but in the company of other strong women who have survived the consequences from infidelity and are standing tall.

"Moving forward" requires courage. "Do it afraid" is an expression that I've heard internationally known Bible teacher Joyce Meyer use. Even when you are uncomfortable, unsure, and afraid, you can still do it—whatever the "do it" is for you. Pray, and ask God for strength and courage. The Lord said that He will be with you. Joshua 1:5 declares, "I will not leave you nor forsake you." So as you move forward, even if you are afraid, rest assured in the fact that the Almighty God is with you. Just take one day at a time, and if that seems overwhelming, take one minute at a time.

"Moving forward" can mean enhancing your look. Trying a new haircut or highlights, altering your clothing style, or experimenting with new makeup can help boost your confidence and demonstrate that you are headed in a new direction. Embrace personal change. Keep yourself up and when someone says, "You look good," don't put yourself down. No matter how you feel you can respond, "Thank you, I feel good too!" Words have power (Proverbs 18:21), so put positive words into the atmosphere. You can exude confidence, not conceit because your confidence is in the Lord. "For the Lord will be your confidence…" (Proverbs 3:26a).

"Moving forward" can mean getting connected with a good, reliable Christian counselor or someone that can remind you of the promises of God and pray with you. Avoid getting a "pity party pal." Also, avoid male counselors. You might be at a very vulnerable stage and you don't want the enemy to take advantage of that. The enemy is so good at catching us in our weakest moments. Counselors should inspire, motivate, and help us to see the good in ourselves. They give compliments too and if you are hearing them from a man, especially when you are not hearing them from your husband, it could arouse "deceptive feelings" in you for that counselor. You do not want to set yourself up for another potentially painful situation. It has happened! It is just not worth it!

"Moving forward" means focusing on the positive. "Finally, brethren, whatever things are true, whatever things are noble, whatever things are just, whatever things are pure, whatever things are lovely, whatever things are of good report, if there is any virtue and if there is anything praiseworthy—meditate on these things" (Philippians 4:8). Stay positive, do positive things, surround yourself with positive people, think positive thoughts, listen to positive music and messages, go to positive places, and speak positive words. Be very careful about what you say. The enemy cannot read your mind but he can hear what comes out of your mouth. You don't want to give him ammunition to use against you.

"Moving forward" means pressing through dry seasons. A week or so after the passing of his father, a friend told me that he had not been able to get into reading the Bible or praying. I have not experienced parental loss, but I have experienced that kind of dry season. That type of dry season can be induced by the loss of a loved one, whether through death or divorce. I suggested that he feed himself "intravenously" until he was at the place where he could "spoon-feed" himself again. By intravenously, I meant that he should *listen* to the Word daily, whether preached, taught or read. Thanks to modern technology, that can happen through many resources. Experiencing the Word that way could help sustain him until he was able to pick up a Bible and read it for himself. When you are in a dry season and find it difficult to read the Bible, feed yourself intravenously—take advantage of technology. No matter the method you choose, just make sure you are feeding on God's Word daily!

"Moving forward" means making time for you. Often, after a woman is married, whether there is a crisis in the home or not, she can lose herself in innocent efforts to please her family. Let me encourage you to "find" yourself. Do what *you* like to do, whether by yourself or with a girlfriend. Rekindle abandoned pleasures or venture into new territory. Do something as simple as visiting an old friend. Read a fun, relaxing book. I found that I was reading for church and school all of the time and wasn't doing any pleasurable reading for myself. An easy solution for me was to purchase a book that was a featured "read" on a TV talk show book club. I enjoyed my mental get-a-way immensely; the book was a blast! Then there is the longggg bubble bath with candles around the tub illuminating the room and soft music filling the air.

Laugh! Find something to laugh at… "A merry heart does good, like medicine, but a broken spirit dries the bones" (Proverbs 17:22). Do *something* fun and enjoyable—just for *you!* I remember watching an episode of a sitcom in which one of the main characters did something noteworthy after breaking up with her boyfriend. She sent herself flowers, and even dressed up and took herself on an actual date. No need to be ashamed of where you are. Make the most of it.

"Moving forward" requires you to let go of the past. "Brethren, I do not count myself to have apprehended; but one thing I do, forgetting those things which are behind and reaching forward to those things which are ahead" (Philippians 3:13). It is more difficult to go into your future successfully with the weight of the past attached to your ankle like a ball and chain. Avoid giving food to the past. What you feed will live and what you starve will die. Perhaps Joyce Meyer said it best, "Leave that *thing* where it happened and go on!" Are you still holding on to or dragging that *thing* with you—in your heart, your mind or your mouth? Constantly talking about the past or reliving it is restricting and it will not change history. Work on creating a new life and live it! Make every day count, because a day that comes and goes will be no more. Don't shine a spotlight on the things that you've lost or are losing. Look forward to and give attention to all that you will gain.

Don't view your situation as a failure. However, I've heard that failure is the opportunity to start again "more intelligently." For our purpose, this statement can mean starting again more intelligently in the marriage or after the marriage has dissolved. Operating more intelligently is a new knowledgeable perspective based on personal experience.

"Moving forward" means leaving emotional baggage behind. It seems like women are always carrying a tote bag of some sort and most times, we really need to. Over the years, I've collected all different kinds, shapes, sizes, and colors. A lot of us women-folk carry emotional tote bags as well, complete with a full filing system. The files may contain records of who, what, when, where, why, and how hurt was inflicted.

> It is more difficult to go into your future successfully with the weight of the past attached to your ankle like a ball and chain.

While we may need to haul our tangibles in bags as we go from place to place, we do *not* need to and should not carry emotional baggage. I know of a woman who for years had experienced significant physical pain because over a long period of time, she lugged various heavy bags to and from work. The harm caused by carrying those literal bags might be more easily diagnosed than the severe damage caused by carrying emotional baggage. Rid yourself of emotional baggage; it may be more detrimental then you realize.

"Moving forward" can mean pursuing your own passion. As a wife, you probably have made many personal sacrifices, denying your own desires in order to support your husband and his vision. Now may be a great time to go after the thing that is in your heart to do. Ask God in what direction you should go, whether it is picking up something old or starting something new. What is *your* passion?

"Moving forward" may require you to do things that you would have otherwise depended on your husband to do. If you also are a person who depended on your spouse to do the "manly" things around the house, be encouraged to do those things on your own. After splitting from my husband, I had to become more independent. When my children and I relocated, I put their bunkbeds together. It was a very heavy set, so I had my cell phone nearby in case I became lodged in between the wood! Sounds funny, but I was ready! Earlier that day, I had taken one of the bed screws to a home improvement store and asked what kind of tool I needed to assemble the beds. I didn't mind letting the male sales associate know that I was totally void of tool knowledge. Normally it's not a good idea to show "consumer ignorance" publicly in any area lest you be taken advantage of. However, I wasn't too concerned about being taken to the bank over a hand tool. In any event, without incident I successfully assembled the bunkbeds.

"Moving forward" can mean reaching out to others. You don't have to wait for your situation to be picture perfect before you help someone else. I challenge you to call at least one woman that you know who is hurting, and comfort her. Speak words of encouragement and assurance. Also, if fitting, talk about the lessons that you have learned. Or perhaps you can just be the listening ear that she needs. Helping others will help you move forward.

So, as you are moving forward, don't get mad, get even. As we have learned from the exemplary story of Vanessa L. Williams, don't get *even* in the sense of exacting revenge, but get *even* through your success, spawned from moving forward!

6

Too Legit to Quit

"We are hard-pressed on every side, yet not crushed;
we are perplexed, but not in despair; persecuted,
but not forsaken; struck down, but not destroyed."

2 Corinthians 4:8-9

In 1991, hip-hop artist MC Hammer released his megahit, "Too Legit to Quit." The chorus, a repetition of the title, became the survival anthem for many. The gravity of any difficult situation can make a person want to quit. Whether you are in the midst of your struggle, are still fighting for your marriage or you have already moved on, finding yourself in the challenge of a new life without your husband, *you are* too legit to quit!

"Legit" is an abbreviation for the word "legitimate," which is synonymous to "valid," "real," and "authentic." Legit can be interpreted as, "the real deal," "cool," "awesome," and "formidable." *Dictionary.com* defines the word "quit," as "to give up or resign; let go; relinquish." Giving up usually seems like the easy way out. For someone with no hope, it is easier to abandon a person or situation, than to deal with whatever lies ahead. However, I believe that a person who is legit is tough and is an unrelenting force to be reckoned with.

Fortunately, the Bible provides models to help us maneuver everyday life. Take Esther for example—ya gotta love her because she was "too legit to quit." She forged ahead when she could have given up. Her story is found in the ten chapters of the Old Testament book of Esther. She was a "lovely and beautiful" young woman who was orphaned in her youth, and through turns of events became a queen. Esther came from humble beginnings.

She had indigenous issues, but she did not have time to waste on feelings of low self-esteem and inadequacies. Her *legitimacy* was predicated on her resolve to fulfill divine purpose, no matter the cost. Also because she was God's woman, which made her woman enough for the impending task. Please take the time to become familiar with her story. It is intriguing, and would definitely make for some captivating reality TV.

One of the beautiful things about Queen Esther is that she did not allow position and power to go to her head. She, who had been "called" to the palace, had not become caught up in the privileges and perks of royalty; nor was she bound by her past. When Esther was made aware that her people were in jeopardy and the challenge came to save them from certain death, she rose to the occasion. She did not make excuses, or say, "This is too hard; I can't do it." *You* may not have a nation to save, but one of the lessons *caught* from Esther's life is, even when the odds are against you, forge on—be brave and don't quit. Don't stop living and don't give up because a situation has arisen.

Nothing in our life occurs by accident. Poor decisions are made, there are missed opportunities and times of failure…life happens; but God is working it out. No matter what adversity grabs you by the throat and attempts to strangle you, know that God is with you. He is holding you up, fortifying you and giving you the strength to not quit. Two truths that I've heard fit appropriately: "It's my *reaction* to challenges, not the challenge itself that can be my hindrance," and "Pain is inevitable, but suffering is optional." When faced with challenges, we have important, sometimes life-altering choices to make. What is your response? Do you choose to suffer? Are you going to quit?

For a long time, I thought that I could not get a prayer through. It just seemed like God was not even trying to hear me.

I did not want to face the fact that I had to go *through* this, and go through it in God's time. There are stretches where we experience trials for a few weeks, sometimes a few months, and sometimes years. No matter the time frame, God hears your prayers and is working behind the scenes on *your* behalf. It is remarkable; our heavenly Father, in Whom once upon a time we vowed to put our trust, knows what we need and when we need it. In the meantime, He is teaching us patience, trust, hope, faith in Him, and even how to love God's way. Don't quit. Keep your eyes open for the lessons, as you trust God along the way!

I have learned some lessons that have cultivated, strengthened, and empowered me so I would not want to quit. I learned that… It's all good—the ups and downs, the good, the bad, ins and outs—it's all good. Why? Because, the Bible proclaims, "And we know that all things work together for good to those who love God, to those who are the called according to His purpose" (Romans 8:28). If you love God, the "downs" are working, the "bads" are working, and the "outs" are working. All occurrences are working and working for your good. The word "good" is commonplace,

> *All of what you go through turns out to your advantage and for your benefit—the sooner that revelation is realized, the sooner a sense of relief may be felt.*

but if we were to look at it a little more closely, we would see that "good" is "profit or advantage; worth; benefit" (*Dictionary.com*). All of what you go through turns out to your advantage and for your benefit—the sooner that revelation is realized, the sooner a sense of relief may be felt.

I have also learned that I must not be weary in well-doing. Galatians 6:9 encourages us, "And let us not grow weary while doing good, for in due season we shall reap if we do not lose heart." "In due season"—who decides when it is due season? I certainly did not have the ability or foresight to know. I could not let the weariness of my flesh attempt to make that decision either. However, I was not in the position to give up or to give in. There are consequences to be paid for giving up too early; you will not get the full benefits of your experience. God will let you know when due season has arrived. Don't quit; stay in the race and God will bring you out on the winning side. Until your due season comes, be encouraged to keep doing well. "Well-doing" includes, but is not limited to, praying, fasting, trusting God, meeting the needs of others, carrying out the work of the ministry, giving of your talents and of course, not quitting. Do not lose heart and you will reap your harvest.

It could be that we feel powerless on occasion because we put faith in *our* own ability to achieve and we don't see any results. Other times we may grow discouraged because we have prayed, yet God does not seem to be moving fast enough. *God is faithful;* He just moves in His own time. I agree with the observation that God is rarely early but always on time.

Be on a mission. With focus, determination, and discipline, many goals can be accomplished. Don't quit. Ask God for strength to see you through to the end. Run on and see what the end is going to be. When you are running with Jesus, the end is always victory! Quitting gives the enemy the victory.

We must "go through" to get what we need. If God just takes us out, we will miss out. We won't acquire that which He intends for us to gain. Additionally, what we endure, God can later use as a ministry tool—I am an example of that. There is always someone with whom you can share your experience—one on one, or from a platform. God uses life's experiences to shape us, and to accomplish His will. However, if it were up to me, I would have chosen a simpler way to get what I needed. My most challenging trial would be having a hangnail or perhaps a bad hair day. What about you? Unfortunately, quick fixes seem to produce microwave results. Many of us have experienced eating food that has been reheated in the microwave. Sometimes the food is not warmed well in the middle and other times it becomes rubbery. Food usually tastes better when it has been warmed slowly, yet thoroughly in the oven. It takes a little longer, but it is worth the wait. When God takes longer than we expect, He could merely be taking the time necessary to get us to the place where He wants us to be.

As time goes by, we get older in the Lord but, the question is, "Have we *grown* in the Lord?" God wants to grow us up and one way He does it is through our circumstances. When times get rough, don't fall apart my sister; stand strong and handle your business. Persevere and keep your head up. Set your heart to be resolute and unwavering. Don't quit on God and don't quit on yourself! In this very spot in the book, I originally wrote that "quitting is not an option," but the truth is that it *is* an option. Be careful not to make that option your reality. That means you will have to make a conscious decision. But the decision is yours to make. Are you going to quit? I urge you to stand firm, just like Esther. Your legitimacy is in Christ, in Whom you can do all things because He gives you the strength (Philippians 4:13). *You* are too legit to quit.

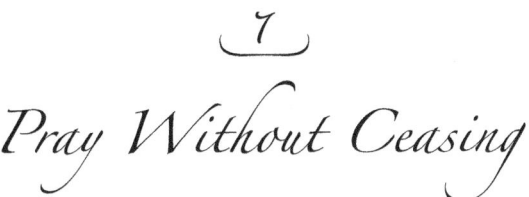

7
Pray Without Ceasing

"Rejoicing in hope, patient in tribulation,
continuing steadfastly in prayer."
Romans 12:12

The Bible tells us to "pray without ceasing" (I Thessalonians 5:17). To pray without ceasing—or ending—is a call to be persistent. It is recurring prayer; a mindset; a lifestyle. It is not only making requests known, but residing in an attitude of prayer, being thankful to God. That instruction may be challenging to accomplish when your heart is hurting. If the truth were told, I didn't feel like praying. I didn't have the unction to pray at all, let alone pray without ceasing.

While I'm being candid, I must confess that I have a hard time relating to those sisters who seem to have it together all the time, even in the midst of a storm. They pray fervently; they utter Scriptures sunrise to sunset; they've got the faith; they are "blessed and highly favored" and so on. It wasn't that easy for me. I struggled with praying. Some days my prayers were short and other days, even shorter. However, knowing where my strength comes from and knowing Who has everything in control, I *had* to keep in touch with God.

As I have encouraged you many times in this book, don't give up. That refers to praying too. Keep praying, and keep trusting God. Pray about praying! If you are as I was, you may not feel like praying. So ask God to give you the strength, discipline, and determination to pray regularly. God desires to stay connected to you on a consistent basis; please don't cut Him off. It is a privilege to be able to link with the God who made heaven and earth; the

God who knows you and your situation better than you do; the God who can fix your circumstances. If He doesn't fix it like you want it or in your timing, He will, at the very least, guide you through it. In the meantime, pray regularly.

God cares about you! The enemy may try to plant seeds in your mind to the contrary. Nonetheless, it is true; God really does care about you. I Peter 5:7 reminds us to cast all of our care—give *all* of our anxiety and burden—to Him because He cares for us. With that assurance, we can go boldly to the throne of grace, and obtain mercy and find grace to help in the time of need (Hebrews 4:16). The great thing is that when we go to the throne of grace, we can drop off what we don't need—cast our care—and gain what we do need. In other words, leave the heaviness, the anxiety, the burden, and the struggle, and replace it with grace, a necessity to forge through challenging times. I like the way Barnes' Notes on the Bible expounds on this portion of Hebrews 4:16—"*And find grace*—favor—strength, help, counsel, direction, support, for the various duties and trials of life. This is what we next need—we all need—we always need."

There are so many things to pray for, that a running list might be necessary. Pray for relationships, revelation, and release. In addition to praying about all that is going on in the world, pray for you, pray for your hubby, your children, your church family…let me stop right here. Yes, please pray for your church family. If they know what's going on, then they are hurting too. You might be surprised at the residual and lasting effect that the breakdown of the first family (or any strong family viewed as an example) can cause. Usually the first family is held in extremely high esteem. They are revered as a godly family unit. Among other things, the pastor and his wife may act as parents for those without parents. The collapse in their relationship can cause people to backslide, to stop attending church, or may even provide validation (in one's mind) to emulate the same behavior. Then of course, there is the gossiping that extends beyond the church walls into the community.

This is damaging to the name of the Lord. So much destruction can occur, that it is imperative to pray for the church family.

Among the many prayers in the Bible, are the prayer of Jabez, Jonah's prayer for salvation, and David's prayer for deliverance. However, the most noted and quoted prayer in the Bible, is the one we often refer to as *The Lord's Prayer*. This prayer, which is also called *The Model Prayer* offers us the key points of prayer. I would be remiss if I did not include this prototype in a chapter about prayer.

Before the prayer even begins in the sixth chapter of the Gospel of St. Matthew, God lets us know that He is already in tune to our needs. Whoop!

...For your Father knows the things you have need of before you ask Him. In this manner, therefore, pray:

> *Our Father in heaven, Hallowed be Your name.*
> *Your kingdom come. Your will be done*
> *On earth as it is in heaven.*
> *Give us this day our daily bread.*
> *And forgive us our debts,*
> *As we forgive our debtors.*
> *And do not lead us into temptation,*
> *But deliver us from the evil one.*
> *For Yours is the kingdom and the power and the glory forever.*
> *Amen.*
> *For if you forgive men their trespasses, your heavenly Father will also forgive you. But if you do not forgive men their trespasses, neither will your Father forgive your trespasses.*

All of the elements in this *model prayer* are important. However, there is one vital point that is mentioned in the prayer and immediately after. Following the "Amen," Jesus goes on to express the importance of forgiveness. If we don't forgive, we will not be forgiven. It disrupts our relationship with God and with others. In the prayer, the part about forgiveness comes with a condition, "*as we forgive.*" Forgiveness is imperative; it can make or break a prayer and relationships. Forgiving can be a tough thing to do, but it can be done. Forgiveness—something to definitely pray about, and do.

You may be aware from experiences that praying doesn't always bring about instant results. God moves in His own time. Consequently, we may not pray as often or as hard, or we may lose patience while waiting for answers. Facing the reality that the results may not be immediate, we must keep praying. Waiting can surely be a nuisance. Generally, we don't like to wait, not even on God. Maybe an inward look would reveal that we don't really believe that God will come through. Interestingly, prayer is not always about the answer or blessings we await. We fail to see the importance of it. The benefits of prayer are many, but please consider these:

- ~ Prayer fosters a closer, more personal relationship with God.
- ~ Prayer invites God into our day and our business.
- ~ Prayer increases sensitivity to the needs of others.
- ~ Prayer gives us focus.
- ~ Prayer strengthens us and sharpens our discernment.
- ~ Prayer makes us aware of our reliance on God's power and not our own.

There are stories in the Bible in which God responds immediately and there are some that attest to the fact that He takes *His* time in revealing answers. Nonetheless, all of the stories affirm the truth that His timing is perfect timing.

I've heard on countless occasions and have read numerous bumper stickers declaring that "Prayer Changes Things." It certainly is a nice little catchphrase. Unfortunately for some, that is all it is. But prayer really does change things. Prayer changes us, too. God can change you in the midst of your circumstances. While we are busy sending God all over the world to do everything, with and for everybody, God is in the midst of transforming us—the pray-er, the interceder. That's another benefit. Prayer puts us in a position of dependency and expectation, with our trust in God *increasing* every moment that we have not yet experienced the manifestation of our prayer. So, don't stop praying—God desires the fellowship and you, as well as others, need *your* prayers.

Worrying is not going to improve any situation. Someone stated so profoundly, "If you're going to worry about it, don't pray about it; and if you're going to pray about it, don't worry about it." If you are worrying, please don't; it's not worth your time. I wasted valuable time worrying about this and that. It didn't change matters, and it didn't hurry things along. It just didn't help. We serve a great big God who handles great big problems all the time. While knowing that, I didn't really internalize it until life experiences trained me. By praying in faith, you can make it through what seems impossible. Put a prayer on it, whatever it is, and let God "do what He do!"

> *Prayer puts us in a position of dependency and expectation, with our trust in God increasing every moment that we have not yet experienced the manifestation of our prayer.*

Before our church disbanded, I had started to attend services at another church. One Sunday during altar call, the pastor had those of us standing in front, pair up and pray for each other. This was at a time when I was still very raw. I was so overwhelmed, I started crying. My partner prayed for me. When it was my turn, I was still crying and never did pray for her. I just cried. I was caught up in me and "mine." I should have taken the focus off me so that I could see and pray for the concerns of the young lady. She responded to the altar call so apparently she had a need too. Where is *your* prayer focus? Are you too absorbed with yourself?

The Bible states that, "The effective, fervent prayer of a righteous man avails much" (James 5:16). So even if you do not see a difference, based on that Scripture, know that your prayers *are* making a difference; they profit much. They have a great return. Keep praying. But of course, prayer isn't just "Give me," "I want," "I need," "Move now Lord," and then just keeping our eyes open for the answers to our requests. Prayer also involves actively listening and being open to hear what God has to say. Sometimes when we are finished praying, it is like we hang up the phone before God can speak. We leave Him looking at the receiver, disappointed that He never had a chance to participate in the conversation. He is interested in a two-way conversation. What is God saying to you? If you want to hear from God, take the time to listen.

During our marriage, I sent up countless prayers—for Andrew and for us. After separating, when it had become evident that we would not be reuniting, I altered my prayers. I was no longer praying for reconciliation, but still praying for a transformation in Andrew's life. I genuinely believed that God could and would change my husband and that He desired to use Andrew for His glory in a way that would significantly impact the kingdom. After so much time had passed, I felt that many people had given up on Andrew and had even stopped praying for him. As hurt and devastated as I was, I couldn't find a reason to stop praying for him. If it becomes difficult to pray for your husband, it might be helpful to look beyond who he has become and see him as God sees him.

I Thessalonians 5:16-18 asserts, "Rejoice always, pray without ceasing, in everything give thanks; for this is the will of God in Christ Jesus for you." Surrounding "pray without ceasing" is "rejoice always" and "in everything give thanks…" for this is the want, the desire, the wish of God in Christ Jesus for you. So while persevering in prayer, remember to *rejoice always* and *give thanks* always. That is what God wants. Well, in case you are thinking that you don't have much to be thankful for, remember that no matter how bad it looks, it can always be worse. But most of all, remember that God is with you. You and I have so much to appreciate. If I were to give you a list of things to be thankful for, you might review it and conclude that none apply to you. So, in that case, you come up with your personalized list of things to be grateful for. And please add to your *I'm Thankful For* list, things that have not yet come to fruition. Be thankful in advance for what God is going to do. He has some good things coming down the pike just for you. In the meantime, and always, do not give up; keep on praying!

8

Support Team

"Blessed is the man who walks not in
the counsel of the ungodly…"

Psalms 1:1

No man is an island…so please, *don't* try to be one. Being connected is important. People develop and become refined because of the interaction and bond with others. Therefore, God looks out for the "lone ranger" by instructing that we comfort, edify, and bear one another's burdens; being connected has purpose. Additionally, Proverbs 27:17 states, "As iron sharpens iron, so a man sharpens the countenance of his friend." Although this Scripture has a masculine connotation, the principle is suitable for all. Having a support team is, in effect, "iron sharpening iron."

Looking back, I realized that I spoke with a few people here and there about what was going on with my marriage. However, having a team of consistent helpers would have been more beneficial. They would be a special group of people to support me, lend a hand, a voice, an ear, or a prayer as necessary—a "Dream Team!"

Over time, the people I received the most help from were my sister, my mother, my prayer partner, and a professional Christian counselor. The assistance was not always from everyone at the same time; sometimes it was different people at varying phases of my ordeal. Each person was a woman of God with her own unique gifting to assist me. At the time, I did not think of them as my support team; but that is what they were. Thinking back, I realize that I did not maximize the utilization of these gifts to my

Support Team

advantage. I could have tapped into their specialties with more exact requests. For instance, articulating, "I really need you to do this," or "I really need you to do that." Just bidding that they, "Pray for me," leaves a lot of room for guesswork. However, understandably, when the heart of someone needing help is torn, that person is not necessarily devising organized plans for assistance.

I am blessed with a mother of sound mind, who is trustworthy and insightful. Yet for some reason, I did not feel like I could tell her what I had been enduring. I don't know if it was due to concern about what I thought her response would be or fear that I had let her and my family down. There could have been any number of explanations. I was sure that the revelation would have a profound effect on many. My anguish was so bottled up inside me, that when I reached the point that I could no longer nestle the secret in my bosom, it was liberating to finally release the pressure. I exhaled. At long last, details started trickling out one day as we were preparing to attend a family celebration. "I didn't think that I could tell you," I confessed to my mother. Effortlessly she responded, "Of course you could have." It was an assertion that I knew was true, yet I allowed something to block me from divulging the secret much sooner.

> It is key to have support, especially when going through an extremely challenging and earth-shaking season.

It is key to have support, especially when going through an extremely challenging and earth-shaking season. You may not realize just how significant or just how vital *some kind* of support is. I highly recommend it, and Scripture addresses the benefit of it.

> *Two are better than one, because they have a good reward for their labor. For if they fall, one will lift up his companion. But woe to him who is alone when he falls, for he has no one to*

> *help him up. Again, if two lie down together, they will keep warm; but how can one be warm alone? Though one may be overpowered by another, two can withstand him. And a threefold cord is not quickly broken* (Ecclesiastes 4:9-12).

So, if you'd like to gather a team, I have some suggestions. First, consult God. Through prayer, allow God to lead your "support-team-seeking" endeavors. Also, think of women in your life who love you, are concerned about your wellbeing, and are completely capable of giving you support. Some of these people can be a part of your team. You may not have a mother or sister to rely on, and that is okay. Who is the next best person? Consider her.

A good support team should be made up of people who give godly counsel and who will be honest with you; people who will tell it like it is. Please be careful from where and from whom you seek counsel (Psalm 1:1). It is not wise to have any ol' person speaking into your life. This team is a group of people who are willing to be there for you and to guide you through your pain and healing process. Your team can comfort and encourage you and help alleviate some of the weight. These are people who will pray for you and with you. People who remind you of God's promises, provide a good listening ear and valuable advice. People who can and will keep your business private. This team needs to be able to tell you without compromise what you need to hear, not just what you want to hear.

Your sisters in support can hold you accountable as well. While vulnerable, your flesh could urge you to engage in "unbecoming" activity. They can aid in keeping you from going off the deep end—if they see it, sense it, or you confide in them. I encourage disclosure. Your sisters are there to help. When you share what is going on—what you are feeling and experiencing—they will better know how to assist you. Having a person or people that you know you have to answer to makes it easier to stay on the straight and narrow. Out of all of my weight loss endeavors, the most successful was the one in which I had an accountability partner. Accountability is essential.

The support you receive does not have to be only for emotional matters. They can also meet other needs, such as help with the children or running errands—whatever support looks like to you. However, if they are not on point with your desires, let them know what you prefer. You may not want everyone helping at once, so alternate people at different times as you see fit. They are all still Team You.

Diversifying your team is a good idea. Different people bring different strengths to the table so you will be able to draw from a range of experiences. Expanding your options will allow you to tap into new knowledge and get additional desired assistance. They may help in ways you didn't think of or didn't think possible.

Someone can be the designated "hype man." Her role is to support you with words of encouragement—"Sis, it's going to be alright, you will make it through"; "God is working it out"; "Keep the faith." She doesn't have to read you Scriptures upon Scriptures; she is there just to give you desired assurance.—I was actually making the hype man comment in jest to point out that not every team member has to be deep. Let your team know what you need—even if it is a hype man.

Another consideration is to just wing it, making connections as formal or informal as you would like, and as frequent or infrequent as necessary. What you do with the team does not have to be structured, but should be regular. Everybody doing what they can, when they can, and how they can. Assess your needs. If you do not know, that's okay. Your team can help you figure it out. As you go along, make sure you are using the resources around you to assist where most valuable.

Some of you may not have access to nor trust many people, so fortunately your team can consist of one other person. I do not want to give the impression that a team has to be thirty people. One person can be there for you to render essential support. If you find that one person is not enough, but that is all you have, start there. As a bonus, they may have resources to unite you with others. When you can, start including others, so that one person doesn't become overloaded.

Right before we got married and before Andrew became a pastor, Nicolas, a twenty-seven-year-old man Andrew was trying to help with his spiritual walk, was intentionally shot and killed. I had started to build a friendship with Nicolas and his wife, so when he died, it was hard for me. During the wake, I was sitting in the overflow area on the side of the sanctuary by myself, tearing up. Lydia, one of the church moms who had befriended us young folk, came over to me and sat down. I believe she handed me some tissue, but that was it. She did not fan me or ask any questions for which the answers were obvious or try to convince me that Nicolas looked asleep. Lydia did not rub my back or even hug me. She just sat there with me. That unpretentious gesture was all I needed. While this particular situation had nothing to do with betrayal, it does demonstrate simple, noninvasive support. You may want or need someone to just sit there with you to be a strong presence. Just in case your team does not figure that out as Lydia did, it is reasonable to tell them.

You may consider contacting and gleaning knowledge from someone you know who has successfully navigated the challenges that come with separation or divorce. Maybe seek out another pastor's wife. Even if she has not endured similar circumstances, she may have a lot of experience counseling on that topic. I had many pastor's wives around me that I could have shared with, but I kept my lips airtight. I was in an organization *for* pastor's wives, designed to be a safe place for venting and support. I could have totally unpacked my baggage, knowing the information would have remained secure amongst us. It's like Vegas; what happens

Support Team

there, stays there. I would attend our monthly meetings and listen to what others conveyed, but I did not say a word. I obstructed my own blessings by not taking advantage of what was within my reach. I knew they could have and would have guided me through some of my uncharted territory. I was the youngest in the group, so I was surrounded by plenty of wisdom in those seasoned ladies. This is what you call "starving in the midst of plenty." That self-imposed exclusion was an enormous mistake. Are you overlooking assistance within your reach?

To the possible disapproval of some, I believe that marital insight can be collected from women who have been divorced, as well as from those who have not. A divorced woman is qualified to offer her wisdom having endured all the ups and downs of her experience. Valuable knowledge can be gained from both perspectives.

If someone you are comfortable with extends an open offer such as, "If you need anything don't hesitate to call," well then, don't hesitate to call. Don't keep having internal debates when you need care and can have it.

Also, please respond if someone reaches out to you, especially if you know that person is trustworthy. By invitation, I attended a special service at Julia's church. She is a pastor's wife that I was acquainted with. At that time, I was really hurting. During the service, I became overwhelmed and started to cry. I was not wailing and drawing attention to myself, but Julia took note. She obtained my address and mailed a card to me. It was a lovely card with her handwritten personal sentiments. I was so surprised by and grateful for her concern, encouragement, and offered shoulder. Yet, for some reason, I did not respond to her. I don't know what my problem was. The very least I could have done was send a thank you note. Who knows, maybe she could have been a part of my support team as well. Words cannot express how much I appreciated what Julia did. It was very rude not to acknowledge her thoughtfulness.

There may be instances in which people want to help but are unsure of what they can do or if they should approach you. If you see or sense that and feel at ease, consider initiating contact. If you know they can be of assistance, tell them how. Be leery of befriending the "town crier." She can lure you in by portraying herself as a good listener, when her intentions are essentially unscrupulous. She has to pretend to be a good listener to get all the good information from you to spread. Be aware!

Also, be aware of drawing a "pity party partner." This person may connect with you because she can identify with your pain, but all she is compelled to do is have a pity party, whine and complain. She's a liability and has the potential of dragging you down.

Most importantly, nothing or no one can replace going to God. I remember a time earlier in our marriage when Andrew and I had a disagreement. I was fuming. My immediate reaction was to call my sister. Well, as God would have it, my sister was not reachable. That put me in the position of *having* to pray. In actuality, that should have been my first thought, not an afterthought. I believe in having a support system, but talk with God first. As Joyce Meyer would say, "Go to the throne, not to the phone." He is your ultimate soother, source, and strength.

You don't have to be an island, suffering alone and in silence. Build your support team, prayerfully seeking your needed assistance.

9
The Other Woman

> "But I say to you who hear: Love your enemies, do
> good to those who hate you, bless those who curse
> you, and pray for those who spitefully use you."
> Luke 6:27-28

"So what's this Vivian got that you don't have? Three tits?" That is one of my favorite lines from the movie, *Legally Blonde*. So, what does this other woman in your story have that you don't have? Well, I am pretty sure that it is not three tits! Who is she? Where did they meet? Is she beautiful? What can she do for him that I can't do? A mental catalog of questions, thoughts, and imagery has perhaps invaded your mind. However, don't become obsessed with "the other woman" or embellish her in your mind. Don't envision her to be more than what she is. Do not concern yourself with those notions. It is a waste of precious time and good energy contemplating any of that.

Becoming consumed with the other woman might be more likely to occur when you don't know much, if anything about her, just that she exists. I knew that *she* existed, but I didn't know what she looked like; that caused me to experience some paranoia. Our congregation was small, which made it easier to spot a new face. So, new faces made me speculate. In addition to church, she could show up anywhere and I would not know it was her. That made me wonder continuously. I can identify with any woman going through this situation, not knowing who the mistress is and what she looks like. Is she a church member? Is she in the choir, an usher or is she bold enough to sit on the pew right behind you?

Is she the grocery store clerk, the bank teller or a co-worker? The questions loom.

I just used the label "mistress" which is an older term for "the other woman." A more modern-day vernacular is "side-chick." You may have heard that. I think that the other woman can be any woman. Some come right from the congregation and some from an assortment of other places. She is composed of the complex and the ordinary; the rich and the poor; educated and uneducated; the pretty and the not so pretty. Despite her background and credentials, or lack thereof, maybe unknowingly she traded her self-respect for intimacy, for companionship, for money…for someone else's man. She may operate with a crafty heart, and lure with enticing speech. These days she might not be characterized by the old-fashioned description—cheap, desperate, and tawdry. Certainly, not all mistresses can be lumped into one category.

I certainly hope that no woman would ever wake up in the morning with the intent to have an affair with a married man. People get in situations and emotional spaces that make them ripe for an affair. Various scenarios could lead to those developments such as working closely together. What is her incentive? Money, companionship, attention, prestige? She may want the spotlight and the privilege that comes with being the pastor's wife. Mistresses who are not a pastor's side-chick also desire the accompanying "benefits"—whatever they may be. Furthermore, I imagine that as she is getting caught up in the romance, there are important factors that she does not consider—or does not care about. These factors include but are not limited to: that the wife is a *real* person; that he is lying about something, if not everything; when he buys her things, it takes away from his children and his home; the consequences; and most of all, that the kingdom of God suffers. *That* is the big picture.

I feel that an important topic to address is confrontation. Should you confront the other woman? That is a loaded question! It is certainly one that you will have to fast and pray about. In addition, it is a question that requires an individual response. I wanted to confront. I believe that one of the reasons that God put the brakes on me when He did is because I was on the verge of doing something that could have been very risky. After finding out her name and where she worked, I felt a boldness rising up in me to go by this woman's job and have a few words with her. That could have proven to be disastrous. My flesh was convincing me that it would have been a smooth interaction. I could just show up, say what I had to say and leave. That plan sounded good to me. However, I must have been in some kind of fantasyland. What made me think that she would allow that to be the end of it? My actions could have opened up the door for retaliation of many sorts. She could have showed up at my job, contacted the church or done something to hurt my children or me.

Again, confronting the other woman is an individual decision that should be made after much prayer. If you decide to confront her, please answer these questions:

What is your goal?

What is your motivation?

Is your intention to do good?

Is your desire to confront driven by a yearning to hurt her or to hurt your husband in some way?

Here are some pros and cons of confronting.

Pros:
- ~ Can "potentially" clarify and dispel hubby's lies
- ~ You become a real person to her
- ~ Disrupt their relationship

Cons:
- ~ Retaliation; humiliation
- ~ Regret; end up feeling foolish

- ~ Her response is unpredictable
- ~ A fight might ensue
- ~ It may create more questions than answers
- ~ She might lie to you

As you can see, there are more cons than pros. Even searching around, I found more disadvantages to confronting the other woman. I will not say that she should never be confronted. My feeling is that if it is going to be done, consider everything, even and especially in the context of Matthew 18:15-16.

Other questions to consider:
- ~ What would you say to her? (Of course, how it plays out in your mind may not be how it will actually play out.)
- ~ Can you keep your emotions in check?
- ~ Would you break down in front of her?
- ~ Will you be relinquishing your power to her?
- ~ Will you lose control and punch her out? (I know you haven't been saved all of your life.) These are all valid possibilities to think through.

Hmmm, what to do…what to do?! I wonder what the virtuous woman of Proverbs 31 would do. You know, that sister really had it going on. But with all of that fabulousness, she too could have become a casualty of infidelity. It could happen to any wife. So, don't take it personally that it happened to you. It is not about what you did and didn't do, have and don't have. His cheating ways are not about you. It is about your husband—bottom line. Sorry, just a sidebar.

Here is another valid question—Have you confronted your husband? *He* knows he is married, but in some situations, the other woman may not. Approaching him may allow the two of you to determine mutually what the issues are, make appropriate changes and work at resolving them jointly. Bear in mind that he is the one that violated the vows. Whether or not you confront her, it would be more fitting to confront him first.

If you decide to meet with the other woman face to face, please contemplate the following.

- ~ Bringing someone with you. Take along a witness who will be praying while standing by your side. Avoid taking the sister that is inclined to pull off her earrings in an instant in preparation for a show down.
- ~ Be ready for the outcome—the other woman may not care.
- ~ Maintain your self-respect!
- ~ Meet in a public place.
- ~ Not knowing her frame of mind (aka "level of crazy"), it may be best to avoid her altogether.

When seeking direction, please be clear, God is not going to tell you anything that is contrary to His Word. If you do not find a specific Scripture affirming what you want to do regarding the other woman, then from what you *have* read in the Bible, and know about God, base your decision on that. The bottom line is, whatever you *hear* to do, if it is sinful, it is not God. Don't do it.

As a therapeutic exercise, to get in touch with and release some feelings, fury, and frustration, write the other woman a letter. Express everything you want and need her to know, how the affair has affected you, your family, and the church, if applicable. Vent in the letter. One catch, as stated, this is an exercise. *Do not send the letter.* You may be wondering why the letter shouldn't be sent. My response is because it might open a huge can of worms that won't easily, if at all, reassemble in the container. In an unsent letter you can really let her have it, tear into her, go up one side and down the other; all probably best not to do in person. Afterward, you can ceremonially dispose of the letter and be free of her. No harm. No foul. No sin.

But, what if she confronts you? Oh, my! Did I just sense someone thinking that she better be ready for a beat down? You are certainly within your rights to respond (not with a beat down though). However, remember integrity, grace, and forgiveness. The meanings of these words are still relevant. No matter how gratified your flesh might feel in doing something crazy, never lower your standards. That is playing by the enemy's rules. Choose to go high—take that high road! Have no regrets—don't do anything that you would be ashamed of later. Don't do anything that your children would be embarrassed by. On the other hand, she may not come looking for a fight. (Don't start none, won't be none.) The two of you might actually be able to have a civilized conversation. Nevertheless, until you know what is what, when you see her, and you know that it's her, call on the Lord—"Father, in the name of Jesus…"

Here are some random pieces of advice that a counselor on a Christian radio program offered: Forgive to the point that the person is no longer an issue. See the sickness more than the evil. Experience a transformation in your mind. Be confident. Don't worry about what she thinks. She has taken enough from you; don't let her take any more. Don't give her power.

The Holy Scriptures address the issue of adultery in various passages in the Old and New Testaments. According to *The Nelson Study Bible* notes coordinating with Deuteronomy 5:18, "Adultery was a betrayal not only of a commitment, but of a relationship. Anyone who treated marriage lightly would also treat his or her relationship with God lightly." This brings me to an important subject—*her* relationship with God.

> No matter how gratified your flesh might feel in doing something crazy, never lower your standards.

Should you even care about the other woman—as a person or her relationship with God, especially knowing that she contributed to the devastation and perhaps the demise of your marriage? As much as you may not want God to forgive her, He will if she would only ask Him, and mean it. Considering your own sin, can you empathize with a woman who has committed the ultimate betrayal, especially when her partner in crime is your husband? God hates the sin, yet loves the sinner. God wants you to get beyond hating the sinner. This is where grace comes into play. Grace—there are many Scriptures and songs in reference to it. You have likely read about it and sung about it. This situation is calling you to *extend* it.

Justin Holcomb makes a keen observation, "Grace is most needed and best understood in the midst of sin…everyone wants and needs grace." His depiction may have been birthed out of personal involvement with a pardoning God, as his statement certainly hits the nail on the head. How would you define grace based on *your* individual experience? So while on your knees praying about whether or not you should confront the other woman, moreover ask God to save her and transform her life. *I know, that is a big "ask."*

When the idea of including the other woman in this book came to mind, I thought about it mostly from the aspect of confrontation. Should the other woman be confronted? However, I found God leading me toward forgiveness and grace. While lighting into her may be our desire, extending forgiveness and grace is our obligation. Despite how we feel about her—the other woman, the mistress, the side-chick—God still loves her. She is not beyond the grasp of redemption.

When we view the other woman from God's perspective, it changes the ballgame. If God's grace is sufficient for all of my crap (pardon the expression), it is sufficient for the other woman, too. What is your perspective? The whole thing is bigger than him and her. Could you forgive her? Will you try?

Some points in this chapter may not have been what you anticipated. If you were looking for validation to give the other woman a *big momma* beat down, to curse her out, stalk her or to seek any manner of revenge, it didn't happen. For the sake of clarity, I am not at all proposing that you two become besties. What I would like to convey most is that despite and in the face of your pain, you try to view the entire situation from God's perspective, and respond accordingly.

10

Freedom to Forgive

> "Let all bitterness, wrath, anger, clamor, and evil speaking be put away from you, with all malice. And be kind to one another, tenderhearted, forgiving one another, even as God in Christ forgave you."
>
> Ephesians 4:31- 32

The summer of 2002 was a period of awakening.

In recognition of Independence Day, I was preparing for the Sunday School teachers at our church to minister lessons on "freedom" for the months of July and August. Among the lessons were, "Freedom from Stress" for the adult class and "Freedom from Peer Pressure" for the youth. I was slated to teach, "Freedom to Forgive."

God was setting me up!

While waiting to sell my goods at a local flea market, I was browsing through the August 2002 issue of a women's magazine when an article on forgiveness caught my reluctant eye. I am glad that it did because the article unblocked my obstructed thinking.

The words were powerful and convicting. As I read on, I began to cry right at the flea market. Reading that article came on the heels of having not told my husband that I loved him, for over a year. I had taken off my wedding ring, secured it in its original jewelry store box, and placed it in the back of my undies drawer. Then I shut down. That reaction was prompted by my pain and fatigue. Perhaps in the cobwebs of my mind, I thought that I was making a statement, taking a stand, but was only fooling myself. I was really in bondage.

I must have had some anger and unforgiveness suppressed deep down within, considering the eighteen-month hiatus from verbally expressing any romantic feelings. After seeing, repeatedly that things in his life had not changed, I shut down emotionally. I told Andrew that I did not have the strength to fight for our relationship anymore. That unfamiliar weakened frame of mind caught me off-guard, as I had pressed for so long. The article helped to unearth my buried issues. I thought that I had forgiven Andrew; I even said that I did—with my mouth. Unbeknown to me, I really had not forgiven him.

Do you have an issue with forgiving others? Did you ever view forgiving someone as a matter of faith? I had to deliberate that likelihood for a moment. Then I remembered a Scripture to solidify the truth of that possibility. Hebrews 11:1 declares, "Now faith is the substance of things hoped for, the evidence of things not seen." Even if you do not see your way to forgiving, forgive by faith. Have faith that you can and will completely forgive. Hold on to that faith until what you hope for has manifested.

In Matthew 18:21-35 (please read), we find the parable of the unforgiving servant. This Scripture passage houses the very familiar verse about forgiving seventy times seven (verse 22). Peter inquired of Jesus how many times should he forgive someone who had sinned against him. Should it be up to seven times? The retort from Jesus was to forgive up to seventy times seven. That is a whopping four hundred and ninety times. However, the amount of times is not the issue, but our willingness to forgive as many times as is called for. That is where some draw the line. As in the case of the unforgiving servant, when it comes to forgiving others, some people develop a serious case of amnesia. Some people forget that they have stood in need of forgiveness from God, as well as others, numerous times—frequently for the same infraction. "If you, Lord, should mark iniquities, O Lord, who could stand?" (Psalm 130:3) Just pause and think about how many times God

Surviving the Ultimate Betrayal

has forgiven you. Now would be a good time to lift your hands and tell God, "Thank You!"

The premise of forgiving seventy times seven, however, does not mean allowing a person to violate you as often as they would like. That would be a gross misinterpretation of Scripture. When forgiveness is warranted, be open to it without your detailed spreadsheet of times forgiven, equipped to tell the offender they have reached their max. Especially in this struggle, be extremely careful not to adopt the mentality of the world, which is not going to see it God's way. The world cannot comprehend forgiving as many times as needed. Thankfully, we can forgive and go on about our business. Scripture does not obligate us to stick around for further abuse. Please note, if you see/experience similar offenses mounting up, keep forgiving, yet find a way to end the cycle.

Many stories can be highlighted in the Bible where forgiveness had been extended. For instance, Joseph forgave his brothers for selling him into slavery, Hosea forgave Gomer for being unfaithful, Esau forgave Jacob for conning him out of his birthright. However, the greatest example is Jesus. He, on the cross, implored God to forgive the ones who put Him there—the ones who hung Him high and stretched Him wide. His plea was, "Father, forgive them, for they do not know what they do" (Luke 23:34). There is no reason why we cannot forgive. We may reason that Jesus is able to forgive because He is on a *different* level. Yes, Jesus is almighty and powerful, but everything that Jesus did was an example of what we are empowered by God to do. He forgives us, showing us what forgiveness looks like. Also, Jesus gave the ultimate sacrifice—His life—so that we can be forgiven by God. Because of Jesus, we can be forgiven; and because of Jesus we have the power to forgive.

Between preparing the freedom themed Sunday School lessons and reading the magazine article, God was letting me know that I had not forgiven Andrew. I had some unfinished business to attend. First, I prayed and asked God to forgive me for not being forgiving. Then that same day, I went to Andrew, told him about my flea market revelation and asked him to forgive me. Isn't that something? I needed forgiveness for not being forgiving. Make an assessment—do you as well?

Forgive your spouse!

Sometimes when a husband is unfaithful, it's a secret that only he and his mistress are privy to. However, there are instances where other people know, like coworkers, friends of the spouse, and family members. Some are accomplices, aka the cover-up people. Forgive them too. Once you find out that others are involved, or at very least had knowledge, it is natural to feel betrayed, disgusted, and enraged—nonetheless, forgive them. Forgive *her* too—yes, the side-chick. When God gave us the "seventy times seven forgiveness guideline," it encompassed all violators, for all reasons, at all times. Of course, when you forgive you do not have to stay linked to that person, nor are you saying that you are okay with what they did. You are operating in obedience to God's Word, as well as dropping that backbreaking load.

Although operating in obedience to the Word of God by forgiving, we don't know how or if the other person will respond; if they will be receptive. Nevertheless, it is our responsibility to forgive. When we do not forgive, consider who is really being held hostage. It is not the unforgiven, it is us. Moreover, not forgiving empowers the other person. It's like they have control over us. When we *do* forgive, it shows that *we* are empowered and that we are in control; we are the driver, not the passenger. Also, the issue of forgiveness is so important that the Bible says, "And whenever you stand praying, if you have anything against anyone, forgive him, that your Father in heaven may also forgive you your trespasses. But if you do not forgive, neither will your Father in heaven forgive your trespasses" (Mark 11:25-26). It is hard to forgive when hurting so deeply, but with God, forgiveness is possible and it is so freeing.

Here's a question to ponder—Can you forgive someone who has not "asked" for it? Listening to a podcast, I heard a pastor state that you cannot forgive someone who has not asked for it. I don't recall his rationale for making that statement. At the time, I'm not sure if I agreed. After some thought, I reevaluated and concluded that, in the case where forgiveness has not been sought, the act of forgiving may not take place verbally, but it must occur in your heart. That allows you the freedom to let it go. Really letting it go means not wishing harm, not hating, not holding any ill will, surrendering the right to seek revenge, and not dwelling on it.

> Having an unforgiving heart will keep you imprisoned, while your "perp" runs free.

Forgiveness does not keep bringing up the violation. When my niece, Anna, was a few years old, she broke a piece of my jewelry. Beads bounced and scattered all over the hardwood floor. I did not appreciate that, but it was not intentional. Besides, the jewelry was fake. Pardon, it was "costume" jewelry. In any event, she told me that she was sorry, and I responded affirmatively. I am ashamed to admit that following that incident, every ear I could find, the story went in it. Poor little Anna heard me recounting the tale of her breaking my jewelry several times. After a while, she looked at me and softly professed in her childlike manner, "Said sorry." Every fiber of my being disintegrated. Even at three years old, Anna knew that her sincere apology should have been the end of it.

As mentioned, forgiveness does not keep bringing up violations. However, sometimes issues resurface, repeatedly working their way into conversations because there has not been any resolution. Maybe forgiveness did not actually occur. That is worth investigating. If you are in that predicament—where issues frequently resurface—find the underlying cause of it, resolve the unresolved, and move on.

In the 2005 romantic dramedy, *Diary of a Mad Black Woman*, a wealthy husband, Charles, treated his wife, Helen, exceptionally bad. He even literally threw her out of their house, while moving his side-chick in. It did not happen instantly, but after some payback and with God's help, Helen came to forgive Charles, in her heart. She was able to assist him with recovery from a gunshot wound that had confined him to a wheelchair. His side-chick had taken his money and was long gone. While on his road to recovery, Charles sincerely asked Helen for forgiveness, received Christ into his heart, and…he wanted his wife back. Although Helen forgave him, she chose to move on and was biblically justified in doing so. Nonetheless, she *did* forgive him. Now some of you might say, "Good for Helen; I wouldn't have helped or forgiven him." On the other hand, some might be able to relate to her actions. Yet others might stay, but with an unforgiving heart. Any way you look at it, forgiving is mandatory. It needs to happen whether you elect to stay or go.

Not forgiving has physical, emotional, and spiritual repercussions. Having an unforgiving heart will keep *you* imprisoned, while your "perp" runs free. Forgiveness is a God-like act. If we want to be like God, emulating His character, we have to long for more than some of the well-known traits—loving, wise, and faithful. Among His other qualities, we should also desire the attribute of forgiveness. Forgiveness can be deemed an act of the will—so *will* you forgive?

Life is short; therefore, it is vital to travel light. Carrying unforgiveness is an unnecessary load. The mere fact that God forgives us speaks volumes to what our response should be when we are wronged. I thought I held in my head and in my heart every reason not to forgive Andrew. But, because of the shed blood of Jesus and the forgiveness of *my* sins, my misguided reasoning has been rendered null and void. You can forgive and stay with your husband or forgive and move on. But the imperative thing is that you, with God's help, find the freedom to forgive.

11

Surviving

> "I can do all things through Christ
> who strengthens me."
> Philippians 4:13

The *key* word is in the title of this book, "Surviving." Differing opinions may form when thinking of what "surviving" means. One might think of it as enduring, while another could interpret it as barely hanging on. Let's look at *surviving* according to *Dictionary.com* definitions.

1. *to remain alive after the death of someone, the cessation of something, or the occurrence of some event; continue to live:*
2. *to remain or continue in existence or use:*
3. *to get along or remain healthy, happy, and unaffected in spite of some occurrence:*

Hopefully we can come to a consensus that all of these are fitting. They hit the nail on the head for describing our objective. Our goal is not to just be hanging on, but to remain alive and continue to live happy, healthy and unaffected in spite of…

Filip Tkaczyk wrote an article titled, "Six Basic Survival Skills." He suggests that the number one survival skill is—attitude. While he was referring to wilderness survival in a geographical sense, that skill is so relevant for general survival in life. Additionally, it is applicable as a sort of "marital wilderness" survival tactic. Mr. Tkaczyk advises, "More than any other skill, your attitude determines how successful you are in a survival situation. This first of the basic survival skills might even determine whether you

Surviving

live or die!…Surviving a difficult wilderness situation also requires meeting many challenges while avoiding panic….By upholding an upright attitude, your chances of survival are greatly improved!"

The writer slid the word "upright" in there. That adjective gives us an indication of just what kind of attitude works best. This disposition, the upright attitude, is necessary for marital wilderness survival. The simple connotation is, a right or good attitude. It looks for the positive outcome.

Mr. Tkaczyk makes some relevant points about the upright attitude. To increase chances of successful survival, please take into account the implication of each of the points. I, however, want to give specific attention to "meeting many challenges while avoiding panic." It is imperative to guard the temptation to press the panic button. For some, such as myself, that can be problematic. When in panic mode you may be more likely to do some

> When equipped with your predetermined disposition you are less likely to go off course when a wave hits.

crazy things or think things that are not true, which can cause you to do things that are not in your best interest. Something detrimental might transpire that cannot be undone—all stemming from panic. I am guilty of hitting the panic button a little too often and have suffered the consequences of my slaphappy hand.

Having the resolve that your attitude is going to be a certain way—that it's going to be right, that it's going to be good, that it's going to be positive—is preparation for the inevitable. By "the inevitable" I mean, situations are going to arise where a choice has to be made on whether you live or die (mentally, emotionally or physically), or that may dictate how successful you will be in surviving these occurrences. When equipped with your predetermined disposition you are less likely to go off course when a wave hits. Therefore, an attitude shift may need to occur—from its current position to upright. Some sisters may need a minor adjustment while others may require a complete overhaul. To be effective, an attitude change or adjustment is something that has to be worked on through daily efforts. Keep positive words flowing through your mind. That is what will be released from your mouth. Remember that the words released from your mouth has consequences because, "Death and life are in the power of the tongue" (Proverbs 18:21a). Adjust your attitude as needed; your survival may depend on it.

Claudia, my boss years ago, suffered an awful experience. She was mugged while walking home. Shortly after the assault, when Claudia left her house one morning, she did not see her car parked on the street. She called the police to report it stolen. Understandably, she was distraught—first being mugged, now this. Well, as it turned out, her car actually had not been stolen. Claudia parked her car in a different location than usual. The mugging caused her to develop a victim mentality. It thrusted her into the wrong frame of mind and her attitude had become less than positive. As a result, the panic button was pushed. Imagine the undue stress and anxiety Claudia experienced. It might have dawned on her where the car was had she kept calm.

These days you might see the catch phrase, "Keep Calm and _____." The blank is usually filled in with any variety of one or two-word directives. I discovered that the slogan, which has caught on like the ad "got milk?®" originated in Britain. It was commissioned by the British Government to appear on morale-boosting posters during the Second World War, although they actually were not used. The original poster read, "Keep Calm and Carry On." That slogan is reassuring and is apropos for those who are *surviving*. It gives two crucial instructions: *keep calm* and *carry on*. That's another way to survive. Go about daily life in a calm manner, not allowing anything to work you up or get on your last nerve—because you know that God is in control. You are composed, tranquil and peaceful. Keep Calm and Trust God; Keep Calm and Move Forward; Keep Calm and Keep the Faith; Keep Calm and Wait Patiently; Keep Calm and Persevere.

Perseverance brings hope. According to Romans 5:3-4 "…but we also glory in tribulations, knowing that tribulation produces perseverance; and perseverance, character; and character, hope." Hope has become one of my favorite words. However, it is much more than a word; it's an outlook. It's anticipation; it's an expectancy. You are not a person without hope because the source of hope is God (Romans 15:13). He will help get you from day to day—surviving *and* thriving. Hope should not be a fad, but continual as Psalm 71:14 conveys, "But I will hope continually, and will *praise* You yet more and more." This verse not only mentions hope but *praise*, as well. The word *yet* tells me that praise is going on in spite of any and all occurrences, thus making praise an essential component for surviving. Praise has the power to situate you in a positive and grateful frame of mind. Focusing on God, and all that is right, makes all that is not right fade into the background.

Perspective plays a role in surviving. Every day is a new day, an opportunity for a fresh start. How are you viewing this new day? Is your glass half empty or half full? Are you even sure that you have a glass? Do you always feel like you're coming up on the rough side of the mountain? Try not to let what you are going through skew your view. Misinterpreting things can induce and intensify stress. Since you have to look on *a* side, look on the bright side. It's about perspective. Don't focus on the negative. Shifting your viewpoint and looking on the bright side is a better methodology. With a new day comes new mercies (Lamentations 3:22-23); rejoice each day because God has made it (Psalm 118:24), and you are still in it. Learn contentment through Christ who gives you strength (Philippians 4:11-13); and considering that things could always be worse, find your silver lining. You may not be able to control your circumstances, but you can regulate your perspective of it.

In order to survive your wilderness experience, you must also stay fit. Staying fit is accomplished by maintaining consistency in prayer, fasting, and studying of God's Word. These three core practices are inescapable—that is, if you want to survive. Consistency comes through discipline. Discipline is the practice of *making yourself* do what needs to be done to achieve your end goal. When we look at the lives of successful people, take pro athletes for example, there is a common thread woven throughout each of their success stories—discipline. Discipline makes a person pursue and keep at it even when they don't feel like it. Be disciplined to stay fit—pray, fast, and study God's Word—that's how to maintain the stamina and mindset to go on.

If you *are* interested in surviving, fortify with good stuff. *Get ample sleep.* God is up all night, so you don't have to be. Moreover, you'll feel refreshed and can think more clearly. *Make healthy food choices and exercise.* You'll need the strength that comes from doing so, and your body will thank you now and when you get old. *Eliminate crazy TV* (Psalm 119:37). Your spirit might be longing for sustenance, so I caution against depriving it with junk food. Fill up on nourishment, like inspirational and motivational messages that will empower, teach, and train you. Reinforce yourself with things that will usher you to your next level, and things that will aid you in surviving the hard times. Never mind who da baby daddy is. Just try to apply that knowledge in a crisis and see if it helps. It would be a scandal to give such power and time to anything that will not build up your personal empire.

If you have not disclosed the affair to your spiritual overseer, yet you are still attending the church where your husband pastors—it is probably difficult, to say the least, to listen to him preach. I have been there. I found myself tuning Andrew out. If that is you, try to program yourself to focus on the message not the messenger. God's Word is absolute no matter who delivers it.

Being a pastor's wife can already be a lonely position. So when you are suffering you may feel like you have to do it in solitude. In order to survive, make beneficial connections with women who can assist you on your journey. (Please refer to *Support Team* chapter.)

This book is filled with key principles on surviving, most of which can be applied by all. They are not exclusively for the pastor's wife, aka the first lady. However, what is unique to the first lady is that she lives life in the proverbial fishbowl; her life is on display. No matter the situation, she's got to survive in front of folks.

There are different types of first ladies, and they too may experience scenarios of surviving in the fishbowl. I recall Ms. Ruth, a former political first lady, who supported her husband in court while he was on trial for drug charges. The scandal made national headlines. During the trial, she displayed what appeared to be a unique coping mechanism. Ms. Ruth was hooking a rug, right in the courtroom, right through the testimony of sworn witnesses. Throughout the entire ordeal, Ms. Ruth illustrated strength, fortitude, and perseverance. Leading up to and even during the trial, it may have been unclear to spectators what her intentions were, other than to support her husband. This was because of Ms. Ruth's strategic use of the "poker face"—"an inscrutable face that reveals no hint of a person's thoughts or feelings" (*Merriam-Webster.com*). However, at some point after the trial, she filed for divorce. Survival lessons to be learned from Ms. Ruth is usage of healthy coping mechanisms, demonstration of grace under fire, and employing effective use of the "poker face." Of course, I don't expect any pastor's wife to be knitting in the front pew while service is taking place…but you get the idea.

I'd like to add one more suggestion. Keep a small notebook or journal of the many blessings God has afforded you and the times He comes through for you. Big and small things, write them down—they all count. Refer to your notes any time you get "blessings amnesia" and need encouragement and reassurance that God has your back. Those reminders will help you over the next hurdle.

Surviving is not about just hanging on. It is about thriving and living your fullest despite your circumstances. Maintain the right attitude, keep calm, endure with a positive perspective, and fortify yourself with good stuff. Whatever comes that pushes you close to the edge—hold on. Whatever you are facing—persevere. You're okay. You're doing good. Keep going. You can and you will survive!

12
By Faith

"For we walk by faith, not by sight."
II Corinthians 5:7

What is the status of your faith? If you were to use a "faith-ometer," at which end would the arrow point? Would it steer toward faith? Is the needle fluttering in the middle or just totally aimed in the opposite direction?

Many times, faith comes into play when we have to wait for God to bring about the manifestation of a desire—the house, car, job, health, finances, spouse, children—whatever the request. Faith is also needed for daily life and definitely through braving the domino effect caused by betrayal. *Merriam-Webster.com* offers these three definitions of faith: "belief and trust in and loyalty to God; firm belief in something for which there is no proof; complete trust." Hebrews 11:1 lets us know faith's purpose—"Now faith is the substance of things hoped for, the evidence of things not seen." Faith is what you hold on to until you can hold, or see, the thing for which you have been praying. Faith is like a placeholder—reserving and occupying the spot until what is expected materializes. Also, *The Nelson Study Bible* asserts, "Faith treats things hoped for as reality." Sidebar—we need to be clear on what reality is these days. This "reality TV" and "alternative facts" era in which we live gives a false perception of reality. Do you agree? What is reality? Reality is truth; it is what actually is. As the root of the word discloses, it is what is real. Faith causes us to behave as if the things we hope for are actually real.

After Andrew and I split, the things I believed in were tested. The fact of my marriage and the church dissolving was difficult to fathom. Those outcomes were not supposed to happen, as I had faith that God would come to the rescue of both. The foundation of my faith was fractured, but thankfully not destroyed. Over the years I had considered myself a woman of strong faith. A superhero of faith, if you will, cape and all. That status was somewhat easy to claim since my faith had not been tested to this degree. Despite my devastation, I was forced to face my new reality, along with the challenges that tested my self-proclaimed strong faith. It's hard to articulate the depth of what I felt. However, since you are reading this book you may already know.

I wish I could tell you that I had no questions for God. I had plenty. You may have some too. However, let me urge you not to question the following: God's love, God's sovereignty, His ability, and His grace and mercy. Have confidence that your heavenly Father is all-powerful, all knowing, extremely capable, loves you, and has your best interest at heart. Furthermore, He is always near.

Yet, when God's presence is not felt, that surely may prove to be a test of faith. We may wonder where He is because we are not "feeling" Him. But, God's presence is about "knowing" and "trusting"—not about "feeling." It takes faith to comprehend that. When we don't know if or what God is doing, we might think that He is missing in action. God's movement cannot always be calculated. He is working behind the scenes on our behalf; it takes faith to trust that. When the time is right, He will bring it—whatever your "it" is—forth. Faith does not require our understanding; it's by faith that we understand.

Some of the information shared with you throughout this book is acquired knowledge based on my experience. Some are after-the-fact revelations I felt God's leading to write. While I am still growing in various areas addressed in this book, the topic of faith, out of all the chapters, is one of the ones that challenges me the most. Here's why...

I've been divorced now for over twelve years and it's been more than fourteen years since selling the house purchased and shared with my ex-husband and our children. Since that time, I have been staying with other people, while praying about and longing for my own house. I have a couple of college degrees and work a full-time job. It's not the best paying job but I am grateful for it as well as the associated perks. I have looked for a suitable house, and have applied for jobs that would increase my financial stability—nothing, yet.

Now, my children are adults and on their own. Nonetheless, I still need my own place to live. It does get frustrating. So much time has passed, that on occasion the enemy tries to make me think that I should take this delay personally, that I am not good enough for those blessings. It is especially difficult when I learn of others who have acquired what I'm still aching for.

There have been several sermons preached in my hearing that declared for my pain, I would receive promises and payments: beauty for ashes, I will recover it all, double for my trouble, and God will restore what the locust took. Additionally, I have read cases in the Bible of people who have endured extensive wait times. In a precipitation-free world, Noah waited for the rain promised by God. Abraham and Sarah, in their golden years, waited for the coming of their promised heir. Then there is Joseph. After false allegations, he waited many years in jail and servitude for deliverance. It is reassuring to know that others have survived God's waiting room, and at the appointed time became recipients of His blessings. Nonetheless, my flesh makes inquiries about when it will be *my* season. I caught my faith wavering a little, based on what did not happen, in my timetable. I was looking at the calendar instead of focusing on God, His promises, and that they come in his perfect timing.

God's waiting room has no time perimeters nor is it discriminatory. His waiting room yields great benefits that may often be overlooked. For instance, the Lord is good to those who wait for and seek Him (Lamentations 3:25). Also and maybe more familiar, "But those who wait on the Lord shall renew their strength; they shall mount up with wings like eagles, they shall run and not be weary, they shall walk and not faint" (Isaiah 40:31). This verse does not imply that *after* you receive your blessing your strength will be renewed, but *while* yet waiting you will be renewed and refreshed. It's in the waiting room that one can come to terms with the fact that God's timing is—God's timing; God's timing is right; and God's timing is worth the wait. Waiting is not a bad thing, as Lamentations 3:26 tells us, "It is good that one should hope and wait quietly for the salvation of the Lord." I believe that in this instance "quietly" doesn't mean speaking in hushed tones, but is a way of saying, don't whine and complain in the waiting room. That negative communication may reveal a lack of faith in the Lord, in addition to a lack of patience and understanding. Faith and waiting go hand in hand—trust and have faith in God's timing.

So, you see, my faith challenge didn't end with surviving the complications of infidelity, the loss of the church, and divorce. I am in the dark as to why my desires have not yet come to pass. But, God has been faithful. I've always had a place to stay and have spent not one single night on the street or in a shelter. Praise God! I didn't expect that getting my own digs would take so long. Nevertheless, I have decided, by faith that I am going to trust Him. Besides, I don't want whatever is not in God's perfect timing anyway. I have come to appreciate and be thankful for the journey. God did not forget Noah, Abraham and Sarah or Joseph and I know He hasn't forgotten me. As I continue to wait patiently, I'm going to let my faith take me to the *front door* of the manifestation of my blessings. By faith, I am waiting for my promises.

In my last message to our congregation, I spoke about faith. The following is an excerpt from that message.

Faith is a word used in everyday life. It is a common word with uncommon authority and ability, the power of which, cannot be compared. Without faith, you cannot be saved. Faith is the shield of the whole armor of God. Without faith, the fruit of the spirit would not be complete. With a mustard seed size portion of faith, you can move a mountain. For the "just," faith is a way of life.

While there are numerous Biblical examples of faith recorded, I would like to shine the spotlight on Peter. In Matthew 14:22-33, Jesus had just finished the miracle of feeding the five thousand with fish and bread. Needing to spend time alone with God in prayer, Jesus sent the multitudes away and He told his disciples to get into the boat and to go before Him to the other side.

When the evening came, Jesus was there by himself. The boat had sailed to the middle of the sea where it was being tossed by the waves, and the fierce wind. It was stormy and dark, but that did not stop Jesus from seeing about the ones that needed His help. He went to them, walking on the sea. The disciples, never having seen such a sight, thought that Jesus was a ghost. But, immediately Jesus calmed their fears. Peter then made a bold request. Be careful what you ask for. How many of you have asked God to increase your faith? Uh! I have. In part, that is what Peter was doing when he said, "Command me to come to you on the water." Jesus gave Peter what he asked for—His answer was, "Come." Faith doesn't occur through osmosis; it is gained through experience. And an experience is what Peter got.

When Peter responded, he did not just "come down" out of the boat; he came down out of his comfort zone. In doing so, he began to walk on the water toward Jesus. However, when Peter observed the severity of the wind, he became gripped with fear and began to sink. The situation dictated his feelings and his feelings dictated the outcome—sinking. When Peter started to sink, he didn't request assistance from those on the boat, which might be logical reasoning for some. He knew enough to call on the only one that could possibly help him. Peter cried out, "Lord, save me." Notice, Jesus was still on the water when He rescued Peter. Isn't that just like Jesus to be in the midst of our situation?

Immediately Jesus stretched forth His hand and caught Peter. "Save me"—I believe in accordance with the Word of God that salvation—help—takes place immediately upon our sincere cry for it. However, verse 32 says, "and when they got into the boat," it doesn't say "immediately" they got in the boat. The word "immediately" is mentioned a few times in these 12 verses. But when they got back in the boat, it was "and when they." The verse says nothing about "immediately." Interesting! So, what do you think Jesus and Peter where doing on the water until they got in the boat? Maybe they just simply "walked" for a little while, because Jesus just said to Peter, "O you of little faith." I believe that Jesus used the opportunity to grow Peter's faith, right there on the water, right there in the middle of the storm. Peter was literally walking by faith.

This whole event is so powerful for many reasons, but one of the strongest points is that when Peter cried out for Jesus to save him, Jesus did help him and he did it immediately. Excellent—we all want instant help, however, please note, Peter still had to endure the storm just a little while longer. The difference is, Jesus was with him in the midst.

Many of us are rushing too fast to get back in the boat. We don't allow Jesus to walk with us for a while in our storm. It is advantageous to learn faith lessons in the midst. And while there, make faith-filled statements, not those of doubt and despair. It is about the journey, not about the destination. Have faith that Jesus is with you at the very moment you cry out for help. Trust God to get you back safely in the boat.

Now that we have taken a sneak peek at Peter's faith—what about yours?

Peter's faith led him to experience a mighty demonstration of God's power. What does your faith lead to? Faith requires action. "For as the body without the spirit is dead, so faith without works is dead also" (James 2:26). The spirit gives the body life and works give faith life. Imagine that, dead faith, wow! Is your faith a corpse? Is your faith 6-feet under—pushing up daisies? It is essential to have faith. *The journey demands it. Do you know what moves God? That's right—faith. As we look through Scripture we find supporting documentation in…*

- *Matthew 9:22—"But Jesus turned around, and when He saw her He said, 'Be of good cheer, daughter; your faith has made you well'" and*
- *Matthew 9:29—"Then He touched their eyes, saying, 'According to your faith let it be to you.'"*

Your faith can yield a lot, or a little. The results may be determined by your level of faith. Are you still in the proverbial boat, fearful to trust God in any or every area of your life? Your situation may have propelled you out of the boat and onto the water. However, your buoyancy is based on your willingness to walk with Jesus on the water, by faith. All of us feel doubt, frustration and fear from time to time, but a person with faith will walk— anyway. It takes faith! Your dilemma probably does not involve a boat but of course, the essence of the message is to inspire "walking" by faith.

When situations are difficult, we must keep our eyes on Jesus Christ and not on our inadequacies or on how things appear. *That is how to maintain faith.* Fear will cause sinking; faith will cause us to walk steady on the water, through our stormy situations. Peering through the lens of despair might stimulate feelings of hopelessness. Nevertheless, remember, it is a faith walk; so look through the lens of faith. Through what lens are you looking?

> When situations are difficult, we must keep our eyes on Jesus Christ and not on our inadequacies or on how things appear.

Hebrews 11 provides a roll call of some of the "Heroes of Faith," in the Bible. Several of the verses in this chapter lead with, *by faith*. Based on that example—let your day start with, by faith. Let your walk be, by faith. Let your testimony be that, by faith….

Let your activities, the raising of your children, and even trusting God be—by faith. I don't know how long you will be on the water, but while there allow "by faith" to be your mantra.

You may experience some very dark days ahead. It is your faith that is going to be key. Have faith in God in all areas, including faith that God will be with you and your family throughout. Have faith that God is in the intricate details of your circumstances. He *is* in control. Keep your eyes on Jesus, not on the fierceness of the storm—and walk this journey by faith.

13

Fear

> "God is our refuge and strength, A very present
> help in trouble. Therefore we will not fear."
> Psalm 46:1-2a

False Evidence Appearing Real. Word on the street is that fear is just that, false evidence appearing real. Some believe that faith and fear are on opposite sides of the spectrum, and that faith is the enemy of fear. While the power of faith is immense, that fact does not preclude us from experiencing fear in varying degrees. When we find ourselves in tight situations, situations that give us the ultimatum to respond in faith or fear, fear fights to present itself. Sometimes fear causes us to question God—His power, His authority, His love and even His very existence. So what is the deal with fear, this false evidence that appears real to us? We just looked at faith, now let's take a look at fear.

Some fear can be regarded as "good," such as the fear of the Lord, or fear that alerts to danger. However, I'm not referring to that, I'm speaking of "bad" fear. The fear that comes courtesy of the evil one. Fear that will disrupt a life, if allowed.

The job of the enemy is to steal, kill, and destroy. One way he accomplishes that mission is through fear. Fear causes people to make hasty decisions, which many times are poor decisions. Fear can make you go off course; you push that big red panic button and away you go, down an unnecessary road. It can have you terrified of situations that may not ever happen. Joyce Meyer stated that "Fear is putting faith in what the devil says." Fear may make you see things that are not there. In that regard, fear is similar to faith. The difference is, faith causes you to see the unseen positives while fear causes you to see the unseen negatives.

Considering the fallout from infidelity, there are many relevant circumstances that can prompt fear. The possibilities are virtually endless. For example: not knowing the stability of your future and finances; raising your children; being alone; losing status and privileges; and retaliation from spouse, congregation or the other woman. A few you may have experienced; some were my fears. Nonetheless, every time you experience a fear, look at it square in the eye and dispel it with the truth of God's Word. Take finances for instance, which may be an issue for many upon separation or divorce. Decree and declare, "God will supply all my need according to His riches in glory by Christ Jesus (Philippians 4:19). God is able to do exceedingly abundantly above what I ask or think (Ephesians 3:20). I am an heir of God through Christ (Galatians 4:7) so what my Father has, I have." Hit the enemy with a single Scripture or a medley of them—dispel the fear of lack, or anything, with the truth of God's Word.

> *Hit the enemy with a single Scripture or a medley of them—dispel the fear of lack, or anything, with the truth of God's Word.*

I can remember a time during our separation that I was obsessing over something Andrew was going to do. The "what ifs," "whys," and "how comes" kept dancing in my head. Then my son, for some reason said to me, "Let go and let God." Hmm! It was odd because he didn't use terminology like that, yet it was perfect timing. The force behind my constant mental attention to that matter was at first a mystery. I later determined it was fear driven. Fear of what, I don't even know. It was totally uncalled for. Fear can creep up in any place, at any time. When fear gets behind the wheel, it is time to change drivers. Faith is a much more proficient driver.

Surviving the Ultimate Betrayal

    Some husbands use fear tactics to intimidate their wife. This can happen for any reason. For instance, your husband may not want you to tell your spiritual overseer about his affair; or if your marriage is heading for divorce, he may not want you to receive what is rightfully yours. He then may try using fear to manipulate you. Be attentive not to let intimidation, whether intended or not, scare you into not doing what you should, or not sticking up for what you want and for what is right for you. What you feel, what you say and what you want matters. Some husbands are bullies, truth be told. Don't be surprised by any attempts to induce fear. If you find yourself in the midst of a *live* situation and your mind is ablaze, you might want to step back, let go of the panic button, exhale, and calm down. Then proceed in the direction your steadied mind instructs.

"Brave" was last year's theme for the women's ministry at the church I attend. During one of our Saturday morning fellowships, the speaker reminded us that fear is a spirit. That spirit does not come from God, as II Timothy 1:7 directly confirms, "For God has not given us a spirit of fear, but of power and of love and of a sound mind." When we recognize it as such, it helps to put things in perspective. I think we are sometimes guilty of viewing the spirit of fear as nothing more than a feeling. When dealing with the spirit of fear, it should be addressed on a spiritual level; not based on feelings or emotions. In Christ we have the authority to respond to that spirit as deemed necessary. Luke 10:19 declares, "Behold, I give you the authority to trample on serpents and scorpions, and over all the power of the enemy, and nothing shall by any means hurt you." I believe that fear is included in "power of the enemy," as he consistently and strategically engages it as a weapon against us. But you and I have the ability to crush him/fear, in Jesus' name and with His authority. Verse 20 goes on to say that the spirits are subject to *you*. In other words, they have to listen to you; they are under your command. Are you talking to that evil spirit, or is it talking to you?

Sometimes the noise of fear is so loud that it drowns out the still small, calming, and directive voice of the Lord. To combat that predicament, I have a suggestion that may not appear "spiritual," but is effective. Tell that noise to "shut up!" What do you tell your children when they constantly nag you, not allowing you any peace? Your initial response to nagging children might be, "please be quiet," but when they get on your last blue nerve with their incessant droning, "please be quiet" can escalate to "shut up" or "go somewhere and sit down." If you can say that to your child, who you love, then muster up the boldness and courage to speak that to your enemy. Tell that internal noise to "shut up!"

Fear has various assignments. It can deter, it can cause delay, and it can place people in bondage. Also, fear sometimes causes confusion. God is not the author of confusion (I Corinthians 14:33). Therefore, where confusion exists, the source is not God. He gives peace. If you are in a state of confusion and are fearful, consider where it came from. Ask God to replace it with faith, peace, a sound mind, and when warranted, clear direction.

As I mentioned, fear can foster the unseen negatives, which can keep a person harmfully preoccupied. However, when learning the enemy's behavior, as revealed in the Bible, we become less ignorant of his devices. Additionally, think about the different ways that fear has had an impact on your life and what tactics were used to propel you to fear. Knowing his "modus operandi," how he operates, will help you defeat him. It will give you the edge. Guess what else is helpful—being protected.

Providing protection is a job for the whole armor of God. Ephesians chapter 6 identifies each piece of the armor. I would like to propose that the armor be utilized as, *Fear Gear*. Verses 10-18 proclaim:

> *Finally, my brethren, be strong in the Lord and in the power of His might. Put on the whole armor of God, that you may be able to stand against the wiles of the devil. For we do not wrestle against flesh and blood, but against principalities, against powers, against the rulers of the darkness of this age, against spiritual hosts of wickedness in the heavenly places. Therefore take up the whole armor of God, that you may be able to withstand in the evil day, and having done all, to stand. Stand therefore, having girded your waist with truth, having put on the breastplate of righteousness, and having shod your feet with the preparation of the gospel of peace; above all, taking the shield of faith with which you will be able to quench all the fiery darts of the wicked one. And take the helmet of salvation, and the sword of the Spirit, which is the word of God; praying always with all prayer and supplication in the Spirit...*

I started at verse ten instead of verse thirteen to encourage you to be *strong in the Lord's might*, as reiteration that the whole armor is needed to stand, and as a reminder of whom the fight is against. The armor covers/protects areas where fear can enter. "Wiles" is not modern day verbiage, but it just means tricks. Fear is included in the enemy's big bag of tricks.

How do we fight against fear? One imperative way is to dress in the whole armor of God. Not piecemealed, but the entire protective gear. Dress daily—through prayer (Ephesians 6:18) and studying the Bible. Don't think the enemy won't mess with you on the days you aren't dressed in your armor. He's ready every day for a good fight, whether you are or not. The armor is not acquired when you are born again. The choice is yours on whether or not to put it on, as verse eleven teaches.

Each piece of armor has its own significant role to play. However, the shield of faith is singled out as "above all." Furthermore, that piece of armor, like no other, is not only named, but its purpose is declared, too. With the faith shield, *we will be able to extinguish every fiery dart of the wicked one.* Fear is an enormous fiery dart! Put that crucial piece of armor to work—blocking fear, as it tries to attack you from any and every angle.

We have established that fear is not from God. So when you feel it, then what? Here are recommendations on how to manage fear:

~ *Recognize*—Be aware. When it shows up, see fear for what it is. Don't label it something it is not or make justifications for it. When acknowledged it can be dealt with.

~ *Rebuke*—This word means "to check," "silence," or "put down, with reproof;" it is synonymous to restrain, reprimand, correction, and the one I got a kick out of is "telling off." Tell—fear—off! You can tell it where to go and how to get there! In Jesus' name! Remember, the spirits are subject to you.

~ *Repel*—Refuse to accept venomous trash talk from the enemy. Throw it back in his face. Let him know that *you know* that God has not given you the spirit of fear, but a sound, stable mind.

~ *Release*—Give it to God. When you release fear, it no longer has control over you.

~ *Refocus*—"Think about what you're thinking about," is an expression used by Joyce Meyer, which forces examination of "the trigger." What are you focused on that is activating those feelings? If you are anxious, what are you thinking about? If you are depressed, what are you thinking about? If you are fearful, what are you thinking about? Redirect your thoughts, steering your focus away from your issues.

Psalm 23:4 asserts, "Yea, though I walk through the valley of the shadow of death, I will fear no evil; For You are with me; Your rod and Your staff, they comfort me." Your experience may seem like a valley or even sometimes like the valley of death. Remember God is with you; He may not deliver you when you want or how you want, but He will comfort you. Although you may experience some evil—you don't have to fear it. God is willing and able to go through to the end with you. So be careful not to allow fear to cause you to stop or give up along the way. Instead of asking for an escape route, ask Him for the strength to make it through. Ask God for *His* strength for *your* journey. The outcome will be better when you are not relying on your own strength.

Earlier in this chapter, I mentioned the theme, "brave," which apparently is pretty popular. I frequently see references to it in various stores. What comes to mind when thinking about the word "brave" is—courageous, fearless, bold, and strong. Please note, being fearless does not mean that fear is nowhere to be found. It is proceeding in the presence of, or in spite of fear. As you gain strength and boldness from spending personal devotion (prayer and studying the Word) with God and connecting with strong women, you will be able to get your "brave" on. Now, come close. I'm going to let you in on a little secret…brave women know that it's okay to cry. You are still brave—tears, running mascara, the ugly cry face, snotty nose and all. So cry when you must; let it all out. I would not be surprised if some of the courageous women in the Bible, such as Esther and Deborah had tear-filled moments themselves.

We are admonished to "Watch, stand fast in the faith, be brave, be strong" (I Corinthians 16:13). To build up your strength regarding fear, search the Scriptures to see what is said about it, then internalize those verses. They will bolster your confidence, and permit you to combat the "wiles" of the enemy with substance when attacked with fear.

I will jump-start your search for Scriptures on fear with these…

- ~ "The Lord is on my side; I will not fear. What can man do to me?" –Psalm 118:6
- ~ "Say to those who are fearful-hearted, 'Be strong, do not fear! Behold, your God will come with vengeance, with

the recompense of God; He will come and save you.'"
–Isaiah 35:4
~ "The fear of man brings a snare, but whoever trusts in the Lord shall be safe." –Proverbs 29:25
~ "Fear not, for I am with you; Be not dismayed, for I am your God. I will strengthen you, yes, I will help you, I will uphold you with My righteous right hand." –Isaiah 41:10
~ "Whenever I am afraid, I will trust in You." –Psalm 56:3
~ "God is our refuge and strength, a very present help in trouble. Therefore, we will not fear." –Psalm 46:1-2a
~ "I sought the Lord and He heard me, and delivered me from all my fears." –Psalm 34:4

Praying about your fears is imperative—it is a must. We cannot survive this life and the situations we encounter without prayer. Lay it all on the table. God already knows, but I am sure He wants to hear from you. I'm also sure He wants to help. Perhaps He would like to speak some specifics to you. So talk, and listen, and allow the Lord to deliver you from all your fears.

14
The Children

"...do not provoke your children to wrath, but bring them up in the training and admonition of the Lord."
Ephesians 6:4

How does all of this affect the children? Differently! All of the drama that derives from family discord affects each child differently. One child might act out while another could become silent or introverted. With other children, you may not "see" a change in behavior.

Keep your eyes open for altered or unhealthy behavior. The children may be encountering a lot; life as was previously known is or will be different. Your family unit may go through an adjustment period however; what kind and just how long it takes, depends. It can depend on you, the children, and the circumstances. When suitable, allow your children freedom to be openly expressive. Try not to shut them down because dealing with their pain in addition to yours is too overwhelming.

When an airplane is preparing for takeoff, you will hear a flight attendant issue many instructions. One key instruction is—in the event the plane loses cabin pressure—passengers are to put on their oxygen mask first before assisting others. That fundamental yet strategic command stabilizes you, putting you in a better position to help others survive. Your being able to breathe properly and stay strong is crucial to assist those in need. Before you are fully equipped to help your children navigate their new terrain, please make sure that *you* are being fortified (many suggestions given throughout his book) and gaining the strength that you need.

The Children

Children are said to be resilient. They are to bend and go with the flow. That makes me wonder, how many times can a child bend before he or she breaks? Children are just like anybody else. They bend back and forth repeatedly and sometimes, they break—even in adulthood. That is why such organizations as *Adult Children of Alcoholics* exist. Those children did not bounce back, but instead they were significantly damaged by the actions of their parents. Anyone is subject to break after a point. I don't know why more is expected of children. Keep in mind, children need help processing what their sponge-like minds absorb. Be intentional about raising strong, healthy, well-adjusted and well-balanced children. Thankfully, you don't have to tackle that challenge alone. Seek professional help along with the love and support of family and friends. The children need as much support as possible and guidance through the heartache and pain they may face.

Marital separation or divorce can cause changes which may be difficult to accept. Nevertheless, whatever your situation dictates, make the best of it—turn lemons into lemonade. One of the challenges that my children and I experienced during the time leading up to the separation was the gas being turned off at our house. That meant we were not able to take our customary showers because there was no hot water. We started taking baths, but I had to boil water to balance the cold water in the tub. Never being much of a bath taker, I made the best of it and started taking soothing bubble baths—my lemonade. Seems like a small thing, but you get the idea. As you are making lemonade, you are teaching your children to make lemonade. Many of life's lessons are caught, not taught. The children will learn from you how to thrive, not just to survive.

A change in marital status can also mean that the children will not see their father as frequently as they used to and would like to. That estrangement can leave an emptiness or longing for dad within them. I believe that is what my children experienced, to a degree. They wanted to spend time with their father. At one point when asked, they could not make a decision about who to live with because they wanted both parents. I didn't understand that in the beginning. I just expected them to automatically choose me, hands down. "Yeah Ma, of course we want to live with you." I'm thinking, "Can't you see that your father is the bad guy?" I didn't say it though; and I would not share the circumstantial knowledge that I possessed. It may seem like a personal attack when a child does not know which parent to choose if they are experiencing that quandary. It's just that typically children want both parents. Don't take it personally when they want to spend time with their dad. They already have you, but are in need of that emptiness, that void, to be filled with their father. Don't deny healthy parental visitation because *you* have unresolved issues with their father. Knowing that there are certain things that children can only get from their dad, prayerfully, gently, and fairly guide them through decisions they have to make concerning him. He matters to them.

I tried to be strong in front of my children, but sometimes the water, determined to seep through my tear ducts, came streaming down my face, finding no rest on my cheeks, not even for one moment. Although needing comfort, my children longed to comfort me. However, I made sure that my hugs were bigger than theirs were because I didn't want to lean on them. That is unhealthy and burdening to children. Young children should never be a crutch for adults. An adult situation should be handled in an adult manner, between adults. In other words, if you must have a shoulder to cry on, find an adult. Your children may try to be strong for you, but you must be strong for them. In doing so, strive to keep the bond between you and your children healthy and appropriate. In particular with your son, as this example comes to mind…

The Children

After Andrew and I separated, someone mistakenly told my son that *he* was now the man of the house. *Yikes!* What were they thinking?! My elementary school son can't be the man of the house if he's not a *man*—1st qualification; not the main provider—that includes shelter, food, clothing, bills, and health coverage; *and* not married to me. To be the man of the house he would have to be all of the above at minimum. It is natural for the male child to want to protect you and the household. Relieve him of the pressure and burden of feeling that responsibility. When the father/husband is no longer in the home, it does not give the male child an automatic promotion to man of the house. No, your son is not the man of the house now.

Keep the children engaged. Be involved *with* them in various community activities, including volunteering. It will keep them occupied and may open them to new interests. Perhaps they can start exploring fields they would like to pursue in college; gear some activities toward that goal. This would be in addition to participating in church-related activities; provide balance. Whatever you do, they will appreciate you spending quality time with them.

In providing balance, it is so important to make sure your children are taught the Word of God on a regular basis. They should be learning in church however, the primary place is in your home. This is an important biblical principle no matter what the family/household configuration is (please read Deuteronomy 6:5-9). I mentioned earlier that many of life's lessons are "caught." One way that children learn the Word is by seeing it lived out in the life of their parents. I know, that puts the pressure on. Just like me, you won't always hit the nail on the head but don't become deterred from trying.

Pray. Talk with God about your parenting concerns. All anxieties, apprehensions, distresses—whatever it is that you are feeling.

Surviving the Ultimate Betrayal

Talk with God about direction for your family. Seek His wisdom and guidance. I didn't get direction from God on some major decisions; not because He didn't give it, but because I didn't ask. Reflecting, I should have. Talk with God about your parenting skills. He will show you how to effectively raise your children. Talk with God about your children—everything you can think of concerning their present as well as their future. And, equally as important, pray *with* your children.

Pay attention. You may have a lot going on mentally and emotionally, but pay attention to yourself, your children, your and their spiritual wellbeing, their schoolwork, their social life, their social media, your household, and the atmosphere in general. Keep a watch on their behavior and if it changes negatively, address it. I remember someone telling me to pay attention, but I did not get it at the time, and consequently I missed things. So much can be happening, especially all at once. If a concerted effort to pay attention *is not made,* many crucial elements will be overlooked, which will be detrimental to the family, individually or as a whole.

> As a parent, it is our job to protect and cover our children, subjecting them to as little of our drama as possible.

Keep them talking. It gives them an opportunity to vent and will reveal to you what is going on in their head. The children may want and need to talk about the situation and about their dad. However, no matter how much they hurt, it is not appropriate to allow them to disrespect their father. My daughter is more verbally expressive than my son is. In her articulating to me how she felt, she began to disrespect her dad. I stopped her. She was hurting and I understood that; and she felt comfortable enough to discuss her feelings with me, which I appreciated. Nonetheless, when the talk started to cross the line, I told her that she could not disrespect Daddy. I had to change the course of the conversation. I didn't want to shut her down, just redirect her. For boys, as suggested on a Christian radio broadcast, who tend to not be

The Children

as vocal, make talking safe, and a requirement. Their suggested verbiage, "I see your anger and we need to talk about it." Of course whatever you "see" (hostility, introverted, emotional, or whatever) can be substituted for anger. Find innovative ways to open the lines of communication.

When it comes to discipline—if you have a child who is not cooperative, consider doing what has been done over the years: start taking away privileges like, the phone, games, outings, etc. Implement what will grab their attention. Be creative; try different things until you find what works with your children. Other parents or even the internet can provide ideas as well. Additionally, don't spare the rod. That's Bible. "He who spares his rod hates his son, But he who loves him disciplines him promptly" (Proverbs 13:24). Whatever correction you choose, administer it out of love, not anger.

As a parent, it is our job to protect and cover our children, subjecting them to as little of our drama as possible. We cannot shelter them from everything, but when they are exposed to harmful events, console them and talk it through. Communicate using age appropriate information. If a situation warrants it, protect by removal—take the children and go.

While I am on the subject of protecting the children, I have to tell on myself. I can think of a particular time when I fell short in this area. My prayer partner told me a few times to protect and cover my children. Each time I replied, "Okay," and I meant it, but somehow I still almost dropped the ball. In this instance, I was not considerate of my children and their feelings. One day Andrew was going to do something. I was determined that he was not going to. Oh, there was going to be a showdown that night. I warned the children of the potential outcome. I saw the fear in their eyes, yet, it did not register. I called my mother and she spoke wisdom to me; just as plain as, "Don't do it." When she said that, the expression on those young faces crossed my mind. I had already seen their horrified and frightened look, but it did not sink in until Ma said, "Don't." I rescinded. I almost had selfishly and senselessly subjected my youngsters to an incident that would have devastated them. It was my responsibility to shield them, not to add drama to their young vulnerable lives. Remember to guard your children when it is within your power to do so.

Protecting the children also means safeguarding them from exposure to inappropriate TV and radio programs, movies, music, magazines, internet websites, etc. It means making sure the parental control is set on tablets and everything else the controls can be set on. Monitor them—the best parental control is the parent in control.

Please tell your children often that you love them. They need to hear it. They need to be assured and reassured of that fact. Tell them and show them. Please be careful not to take your frustrations out on them. If it happens, don't beat yourself up, but the children deserve a sincere apology. Also, assure your children that the break up, or whatever it is that is going on with your marriage, is not their fault. Some children actually believe that they are the cause of parental discord. They don't need to carry the load of thinking that they are.

I don't tout myself as an authority on raising children, but I do know that it is not good to allow children to be rude and disobedient, even when they are hurting. It takes consistent parenting and correction to keep them on track. Admittedly, consistency was not an area that I had perfected. However, I recognize the importance and benefits of it; therefore, I am encouraging you to stay the course. Remember you are accountable to God for your parenting, or the lack thereof. You may not always be able to permit your children to keep up with their friends or societal norms, as they would like. Be okay with that because the goal is to raise them in line with God's Word, not the ways of the world.

It has been said that when a man says, "No," the answer is "no." But when a woman says, "No," it can be interpreted as, "Let's negotiate." Help your children understand that "no" means "no" and when you say it, that is what you mean. Additionally, it is vital to catch and correct poor conduct as it occurs, so the unwanted behavior does not become woven into the fabric of your daily life. It will be more challenging to deal with later. Correcting undesirable behavior is always in order.

If you are a passive—lifeless, inactive, unresponsive, sit back and let whatever happens happen kind of person—please pray about that. Ask God to help you be assertive, on top of matters, proactive when required and responsive as necessary. No parent in this day and age can afford to take an inactive, backseat approach to parenting. Our youngsters are exposed and susceptible to too many dangers, in the natural and in the spiritual. The enemy is eager and always conspiring to mess over and damage children while they are young and vulnerable. That is easier to do when their parents are docile, weakened, and not on guard.

Use life's teachable moments. What are you experiencing that you can grab the lesson from and say to your children that this is what I am learning? What can they learn from what they are facing? And, as children often do when given a directive, question "why," you might choose to respond, "Because I love you!" instead of "Because I said so." I grabbed that tidbit from somewhere and felt it significant to pass on to you.

Be careful not to be so absorbed in your own pain that you overlook your child's pain. Ask how they are doing regularly and listen to their answer. Respond to their answer. While you may be preoccupied trying to figure you and your situation out, be watchful not to put your children on autopilot, whether intentionally or unintentionally. Be mindful that inattentiveness leaves them to fend for themselves. That can turn out to be a mess. If they cannot have both parents, they should at least have one of you. I am not at all suggesting that being available for your children while navigating your journey is easy and without its challenges, but you must be aware of their needs and vulnerability.

The Bible admonishes us to "Train up a child in the way he should go, and when he is old he will not depart from it" (Proverbs 22:6). If after your best efforts, your child still does not turn out as you had hoped and prayed, do not blame yourself. Everyone has their own journey in life and some roads are rockier than others are. Trust that God still has His hand on your child's life and that your efforts were not in vain. As they grow up, they are going to and have to make their own decisions. I did. How about you? Some decisions were good and some not so much. The trials and tests that your children endure make them who they become and will add substance to their testimony. Many times, a ministry is birthed out of what one goes through. God does not waste experiences. Don't be discouraged. God has all things in control.

When I first started writing this book my children were young, like junior high-ish. By the time I returned to writing and completed the manuscript, they were adults. Somewhere in between, my daughter became pregnant and had a baby at the age of 18. That absolutely paralyzed me. I cannot even articulate how devastated I was. How could it happen?! I was very active in her and my son's life, and raised them in the fear of the Lord. I talked with them, and exposed them to knowledge. I was not perfect, but I was present, I was involved. While teenage pregnancy happens, it had never happened to us, nor did I expect it to. The awareness of the frequency of occurrences did not lessen my pain. I felt like a complete failure as a single mom. I was so shattered that I lost focus. Losing focus was not good, especially since I had another child to consider. Please try not to let anything throw you off your parental course. Press through situations as they arise, trusting God all of the way, no matter what it looks like. Nothing is a surprise to God, so when life happens to you—trust Him!

Provide stability! I cannot emphasize the importance of this point enough. I found that my children really needed to be assured that I was going to be there for them, and that I was not leaving too. I promised them as often as they needed to hear it. After a while, it was no longer a concern so they stopped asking. They could see for themselves that I meant what I said. In addition, I wasn't busy trying to prove to myself or others that I could get someone, too. I did not have men traipsing in and out of my life. My children needed my attention, which was of more importance to me.

One thing I do wish that I had done was to allow my son to spend time shadowing positive male role models. That exposure may have helped his transition to manhood. That mentor could have aided him in areas that only men can foster. I mentioned to a couple of men, people I totally trusted, to call Andrew, Jr. when they were doing *manly* things, but they didn't contact him, and I didn't follow up. However, when I was buying a car, I brought my son along so that he could learn the ins and outs of the process from the men that I asked to help me with the purchase.

Choose your battles wisely. Do not make little things, big things. Life is complicated enough. Your life and the lives of your children will be more peaceful without a lot of needless struggle. Give and take, make reasonable compromises, agree to disagree. That might make life a little less stressful.

There are so many things that can be discussed when it comes to the children. I am not able to address them all. Some experiences are on-the-job training, in which you will figure things out and learn as you go. Generally, children have a lot to deal with—things at home, school, and all that is going on in the world.

Remember to pay attention! Be healthy for you and for them. It can be challenging to keep yourself together *and* the children, but you can do it. Don't give up. Pray, pray, pray and when you finish praying, pray some more. You can do all things through Christ; He will give you the strength. You will survive.

15

Legally Speaking

"Plead my cause, O Lord, with those who strive
with me; Fight against those who fight against me."
Psalm 35:1

On May 27, 1989, I married my love. The day started off rainy, but by nuptials time, it was beautiful and sunny. Our bridal party was twenty-six people strong with the groomsmen clad in black tuxedoes and the bridesmaids adorned in pastel hues. After the wedding and a reception of at least two hundred fifty guests, we jetted off to honeymoon in Orlando, Florida. We returned a week later to "officially" begin our lives together.

During the ceremony, I pledged my love and commitment, for richer or poorer, in sickness and in health, for as long as we both shall live, and Andrew vowed the same. I had no foresight of what would transpire some thirteen years later.

ME vs. HIM

I found myself in court, with my spouse as my opponent. Who would have thought?!

The first time that we appeared before the judge for the divorce, we had several issues on the table that we could not work out privately. We had hoped that the judge would just rule on the issues, but she didn't bother with the small stuff and sent us to mediation. Over the following month and a half, we met with a mediator a few times to resolve matters like our jointly owned vehicle, car insurance, health insurance, retirement benefits, and our joint charge card bill. Additionally, child custody issues were decided in mediation. We agreed that I would have sole physical custody—our two children lived with me, and joint legal custody—we both could make decisions (educational, medical, etc.) for the children.

At the time that I was contemplating divorce, my medical insurance coverage was under Andrew's plan. Medical coverage was a big issue; I did not want to be without it. I learned that a spouse could receive coverage for up to thirty-six months after the divorce, through COBRA (Consolidated Omnibus Budget Reconciliation Act). Thirty-six months of coverage sounded good to me but little did I know, with COBRA I would still have to pay the premium. Finding that out was disappointing news. Since I was required to pay, I did not go with that option. Had I known earlier that I would have to be doling out money, we could have settled our differences sooner. Medical insurance was one of the things I was holding out for. If you do not have your own insurance plan, find out from your husband's health insurance provider and/or benefits department if you can receive COBRA coverage. However, note, under this plan you may be required to pay the entire premium. Become familiar with COBRA rules, and check other options before making a decision. Do your research. Ask specific applicable questions to find out pertinent information.

Please do not sign away benefits that you can have, in a settlement, unless you are fully aware of what you are doing and you want to. Think twice before freely giving up any benefit that you are entitled to and may need now or in the future. Furthermore, know what you want and need, and ask for it. You may or may not get it, but at least ask. Don't allow intimidation or weariness to rule your decision making.

The whole time that you are going through your experience, you might think, "I can't believe that I'm going through this." Unfortunately if you are, you are. It is real; press past the disbelief and do what you must do for yourself and your children. To aid in keeping you sane, it would be helpful to meditate on Scriptures that emphasize peace such as Isaiah 26:3—"You [the Lord] will keep him in perfect peace, whose mind is stayed on You, because he trusts in You." Some of your peace of mind may come from the simplicity of having a plan. Part of my fear arose from not knowing in which direction I was headed. Identify what you are going to do. Pinpoint your plan. If you do not know what you are going to do, don't panic. At the very least, know that you are going to ask and trust God for wisdom and direction (Proverbs 3:5-6).

My feathers were ruffled because I felt that I should not have to be going to court to take care of issues that really should not have been issues. I was frustrated, angry, and stressed. I was in need of the peace of God that passes all understanding (Philippians 4:7). I thought, if only I could fast for it and presto, change-o, I would have peace. In real life, that is not how it happens. No surprise there. Real peace comes as a result of trusting God and believing that no matter what it looks like around you, God is in control.

Educate yourself. Become familiar with the laws in your state concerning separation, divorce, and child and spousal support, preferably before you separate so that you know your legal options, and what to expect. Of course, resources are available online, but going to the courthouse will also be beneficial. There you should be able to get materials and talk to as many people as you need to. With so much information offered online, however, I suggest calling to verify that they do still have paper brochures obtainable before going there. Do as much investigating as you can, because increasing your legal knowledge will lessen your chance of being taken advantage of, by the system or by your spouse.

> *Real peace comes as a result of trusting God and believing that no matter what it looks like around you, God is in control.*

You can get an attorney or file the necessary papers yourself. Ascertain if there is some kind of family court self-help center, which offers free, general legal information for unrepresented people. Additionally, the Bar Association in your state may offer pro se divorce or custody clinics. They may be able to connect you with an attorney through a pro bono program based on your income.

I suggest that as with any attorney, you stay on top of them, but particularly one who is offering services free of charge, as you may not receive the same treatment as a paying client. I found an excellent Christian attorney through an annual publication of a Christian business directory. On a couple of occasions, she provided me with good counsel over the phone at no charge. Unfortunately, I could not retain her as my attorney because of her fee. It may be worth your while to search around for different avenues of professional trustworthy assistance. If you work for an organization that has an Employee Assistance Program (EAP), you may be able to get legal advice (and help with other personal concerns) through them.

If you are being abused physically, get out! Don't worry about what the congregation or anyone else will think. Do what you need to do for you! There *is* help available. Through the court, I found out about the battered women's services. They even had a law office right at the courthouse, thoroughly equipped with resources and assistance. I discovered that these folks are uncompromising about their mission to render support, and will do all within their power to keep your business confidential, especially from your spouse. Please note, although I learned about this service, I was not battered.

If you are going to file any kind of charges against your husband in which he will need to be served, be serious and firm about your decision. I also found out firsthand that U.S. Marshals are very serious about their work. I am not pointing this out to frighten or discourage you, but to caution that you cannot be wishy-washy about your choice to have your husband served—they don't play! So if you are going to do it be prepared to go all the way through.

After calling the police on Andrew one evening over a disagreement about him wanting to take our daughter somewhere, the officer suggested that I go to the court to file for custody. Since at that juncture neither of us had official custody of the children, Andrew had just as much entitlement as I did. I was unaware that I could seek temporary custody. That would have worked in my favor that night Andrew took our daughter from the house. I don't believe he would allow her to be in physical danger, but she was in a situation that seemed inappropriate for her. Armed with the order, he would not have been able to take her away. If necessary, find out if you can receive temporary custody until a permanent order is set. Thankfully my child was not in danger, but if yours is, Lawyers.com makes the following assertion, "If your child is in danger from the other parent, you can go to your county courthouse and request emergency temporary custody. Depending on the laws in your county, you may or may not have to appear before a judge."

Since you don't know just how complicated your situation may get, it would behoove you to gather evidence—pictures, copied documents, receipts, and recorded events, including dates and times. Don't become crazed but cover yourself. It is better to have too much saved information than not enough! Be prepared for the worst-case scenario. Depending on your circumstances, i.e. you are planning to separate, it may also be wise to store your important papers and documents, (birth/marriage certificates, insurance info, dental/doctor records, etc.) in a separate location along with the affair evidence. Don't forget any documents that have both of your names on them, like bills, charge cards statements, vehicle, house, and taxes. Keep records in a safe place so they will not mysteriously disappear.

Months before we sold our house, I removed all important information, with the exception of our joint charge card file. If

I had the file with the monthly statements, I would have had proof for the court showing the specifics. Having evidence of who incurred what charges may have made a difference in how the payment responsibility was divided. The judge did inquire as to who made the charges. However, since both of our names were on the account and no statements were presented the judge declared it equal responsibility. I am inclined to believe it would have been beneficial to me to have been prepared with the statements. Have a copy of all records with your name on it!

File as soon as you can. Also, in reference to child support, you might want to ascertain if you need to save receipts of all money that you spend on your children. I saved receipts, however the burden of proof was on Andrew to show that he was providing for his children. Until an amount of support has been determined by the court, see if you are able to get temporary child support. Sidebar—different personnel may tell you different things. If you don't get the answers you need, call later and talk with someone else. Some people just have more information, or the previous person may have misunderstood your needs.

If you are in a financial crisis—whether your husband is in the home and not helping or he is out of the home—find out if you can obtain temporary assistance.

Do you qualify for alimony? Find out. Learn what circumstances make you eligible and if you can get it while you are separated. If you plan to seek alimony, now more commonly known as spousal support, please research what paperwork you need to provide to the court. I wanted support, as was properly documented on the initial paperwork that I submitted. We had to stand before the judge on at least two occasions. It wasn't until the judge was ready to address the spousal support issue that she told me that I needed to provide X (I'm not being secretive; I don't recall the specific request). Well, I was not prepared because I had not been informed previously that I would need that information. That was unnerving. The judge knew that I was representing myself. I was not a lawyer. I was not familiar with what would be needed, or I would have been equipped with it. I felt like that was something she should have mentioned sooner—*and I didn't ask.* However, the judge was willing to allow a new court date at which time I could present the documents, but I was through. I was anxious to get it all over with and I felt my chances of actually getting spousal support were slim. Thanks to mediation, everything else was in place so at that point I decided not to pursue it. I was just so ready for the divorce. I didn't know if I would be granted anything, but in hindsight I wish that I had powered through and tried. Waiting a few more months would not have hurt me. I definitely encourage seeking spousal support. If you are entitled to it, hang in there and get it.

The entire process can be both physically and emotionally draining, which is understandable. Pray throughout the process for wisdom and direction. Also pray for God to strengthen and refresh you. If you cannot pray, call someone to pray with you. It's perfectly "legal" to request help.

Please consult an attorney and other professionals as needed. I cannot emphasize enough how important it is to become familiar with the law. Search reliable websites to get pertinent information, or make that pilgrimage to the courthouse; but get the information. Knowledge is power. We didn't discuss scams but be mindful of them especially when checking online resources. The vulnerable are easy prey. Seek the applicable services that will meet your needs. Explore your options; weigh them and prayerfully proceed. Be encouraged! God is with you. Let Him fight your battles. You already have the victory; you are just walking it through.

16

A Word of Encouragement

*"I will praise You, for I am fearfully and
wonderfully made; Marvelous are Your
works, and that my soul knows very well."*

Psalm 139:14

Clueless! I really believe that a lot of men are simply clueless when it comes to realizing how much women are affected by their unfaithfulness. The experience is catastrophic and the array of emotions felt is startling. Negative feelings toward yourself can invade your mind—the list could pile high. Have *you* had negative feelings toward yourself during this ordeal; or struggled with feelings of insecurity? Chances are that you have, those feelings are real. Nevertheless, be assured that your husband, or what he says about you categorically *does not* define who you are or your value. Your worth is in the Lord.

It is God that gives you significance and validates you. You did not become valuable because you married your husband; you already had it going on. God has a plan just for you; the blueprint was designed and drawn up before you were even conceived (Jeremiah 1:5). Your purpose did not become consummated on your wedding day; it was preset. While you may work alongside your husband, you are an individual with your own God-given talents and mission. That makes *you* someone special.

If your husband is hurling malicious insults at you, try not to take them personally, let them roll off. Do not accept, welcome or embrace them; don't allow them to become a part of you. Know that those awful words are not who and what you are. He is not seeing things as he should. Remember that his words are not God's words nor are they the last words. Your hubby doesn't have the final say about you. Additionally, beware of falling into the mindset that if your husband does not love you, that you are not lovable. That is far from the truth. Your family and friends will verify that.

Not only do your family and friends love you, God loves you too. Moreover, Isaiah 54:5 affirms, "For your Maker is your husband, The Lord of hosts is His name; and your Redeemer is the Holy One of Israel; He is called the God of the whole earth." As our Maker, God knows us inside and out; He knows the intricate details of our being. As our husband, God offers protection, financial stability, leadership, and unconditional love. As Redeemer, He is rescuer and liberator. As God of the whole earth, He has every earthly thing under control. He is all of those things and more, because He loves you and knows your worth.

God also knows that you are a beautiful creation—your complex inner workings and your resplendent exterior—because that is how He formed you. David describes it as "fearfully and wonderfully made." In Psalm 139:14 he proclaims, "I will praise You, for I am fearfully and wonderfully made; marvelous are Your works, and that my soul knows very well." As I scanned various translations to get a better understanding of *fearfully*, I came across, marvelously, amazingly, awesomely, remarkably, and unique creation. It is more beneficial to feed on and absorb those words. That is what God made you to be. This fourteenth verse expresses such confidence, boldness, and conviction. Speak those symbolic words about yourself with the same conviction, and spice it up with a little "attitude." I am marvelous! I am amazing! I am a unique creation! God did not mess up or make a mistake when He made you. *The Nelson Study Bible* expresses my favorite, "I am an awesome wonder." If you are going to call yourself anything, start with that. Moreover, don't forget to do as David did…praise God for who *you* are—a designer original.

While it is great to get reassurance from others, we are not always going to find that external affirmation, especially when it is desired most. Sometimes it is mandatory to encourage yourself in the Lord, as exemplified by David. Finding himself in a quandary, he was greatly distressed because the people were talking about stoning him. That unquestionably sounds like a situation where reassurance and inspiration were warranted. Consequently, "David strengthened himself in the Lord his God" (I Samuel 30:6). Other translations use the word, "encouraged." Fortunately, David was fortified and able to invigorate, inspire, and motivate himself because of his experiences and relationship with God. This brings to mind the importance of making ongoing spiritual deposits—getting and hiding affirmations from the Bible in your heart—so you can make withdrawals when needed.

If you don't already, it would be a good idea to start saying daily uplifting, stimulating, and reassuring affirmations to yourself. When you rise, while driving, cooking, and before going to bed—squeeze one in whenever possible. Also, use positive reinforcements by way of visual aids—post words, mottos, poems, and Scriptures around so you can be edified whenever you see them. Look in the mirror and vocalize those positive statements, inserting your name as applicable. Speak these pronouncements by faith and aloud—so they can be heard by you *and* the enemy. I suggest declaring them by faith if down inside you don't believe them yet—speak them anyway. Belief will come. Do not have self-degrading conversations with yourself or with anyone for that matter. "I'm not this" and "I'm not that." Nope, nothing of the sort. Stick to what is inspiring and boosting. The power of declaring and speaking goes back to creation…God spoke it…and it was so. So…speak life, speak victory, speak hope.

~ I am an awesome wonder. (Psalm 139:14)
~ I am more than a conqueror. (Romans 8:37)

A Word of Encouragement

- ~ I don't believe what Satan says because he is a liar and father of lies. (John 8:44)
- ~ I walk by faith. (II Corinthians 5:7)
- ~ I have the victory. (Deuteronomy 20:4)
- ~ I have the peace of God. (Philippians 4:7)
- ~ I am the head and not the tail. (Deuteronomy 28:13)
- ~ I am strong in the Lord and in the power of His might. (Ephesians 6:10)

Strength is one of the virtues of the wife in Proverbs 31. Verse 17 proclaims, "She girds herself with strength, and strengthens her arms." I believe that she wore it as clothing (talk about a designer original). To be strong or to have strength is to be empowered. It is having the determination and the will to push through. It is trusting God and exercising faith muscles. It is not being deterred or intimidated by issues or situations. Many of us are still growing in this area, yet we often have more strength than we realize. It inconspicuously builds up in us over time through various tribulations, and through studying God's Word, then asserts itself at the right moment. You *are* strong because God indeed gives strength to His people (Psalm 29:11).

I cannot omit Nehemiah 8:10, while on the subject of strength. "Do not sorrow, for the *joy* of the Lord is your strength." Joy is significant. It is, as defined by *Dictionary.com*, "the emotion of great delight or happiness caused by something exceptionally good or satisfying; keen pleasure; elation." One thing about joy is that it doesn't care what's going on around you; it is not phased; it is going to rise to the occasion. Joy is time-enough—just right—for any situation. It is possible to have a fluctuating temperament based on crazy talk that hubby verbalizes to you, making it hard to stay on an even keel when listening to that nonsense. However, joy can be a regulator; it can help you stay balanced. If you are in need of joy, it is not for purchase at your favorite outlet store. It is acquired by being in the presence of the Lord. That's where

Surviving the Ultimate Betrayal

fullness of joy is located (Psalm 16:11). *He* is the "something exceptionally good."

The famous literary quote, "To Thine Own Self Be True," has been used in a multiplicity of ways, for an assortment of reasons. I believe it calls for introspection to determine who you are authentically and to be that person, no matter what. Who is the true you? Do you still know her? Are you being true to her? Life, as well as the crazy talk from hubby, previously mentioned, can be a distraction, and has the potential to steer you off-course. If internalized, it can convince you of untruths. Have you become so beaten down and unfocused that you are no longer the true you? The you that you were created to be—that awesome wonder. What are your goals? Have the distractions derailed you from reaching for them? Have the distractions changed your perception and direction? If that is the case, I urge you to take measures to get back on track. To thine own self be true!

> *God can masterfully orchestrate what we consider failure and make something good of it.*

If your marriage does not work out, you have no reason to walk in shame or condemnation. Hold your head high and "keep on keeping on." Condemnation is a defeatist mentality from the enemy. Please note, I purposely did not use the word "failed." If you love the Lord and are called according to His purpose, there is no failure (Romans 8:28). God can masterfully orchestrate what we consider failure and make something good of it. Be mindful that He does not operate under time constraints. So, the "something good" might come immediately, or soon, or in while. If a wait is involved, trust that God is working everything together for your good.

When it takes time to see the results of your prayers, rest confidently. God has not forgotten you, nor will He ever leave you (Hebrews 13:5). Don't get down and out, and all "woe is me." He

A Word of Encouragement

knows the aggravation and frustration that you feel. Sister, if you feel like giving up and giving in…if you want to turn your back on God because you "feel" like He has turned His back on you—don't! I am compelled to reiterate, God has not forgotten you. Expect and watch for the special things He does for you, especially the "small" victories and blessings. God has a way of showing up in "the small" to let us know that He is still there. Always thank God for the victories and blessings—large or small.

Years ago, I was at a church where a timely prophetic word from the Lord came through one of the preachers. As I thought about the prophecy during a quiet moment, God illuminated it for me. The word was, "My hand is on your heart." The insight was, God is holding my heart together while healing it; He is shielding it from bruise and break; He is regulating it and will fix any irregularities. Also, He is feeling my heart. He feels what I feel, the very beat of it. What an encouraging word it was. That message gave me reassurance and solace. Fortunately, the same word is for you. When God has His hand on your heart it is being mended, it is protected, God will fix the irregularities and He feels what you feel. God's hand is awesome and it is powerful. Take comfort in knowing God's hand is on your heart.

Allow me to interject some points about being bitter since we talked earlier about internalizing feelings. Bitterness can be a result of mistreatment. It is a real feeling and one that can slip into the crevices of your being if you are not watchful. "Don't be bitter, be better" is an often used motto. "Better" means an improvement has occurred; you are not where you were. When you are better, you are on the *come-up*. And when on the come-up, you don't have time for bitterness. It is destructive and will hurt you and those around you. While I experienced various feelings, fortunately one of them was not bitterness. Interestingly, when talking with two men on different occasions I expressed to each of them that I did not want to marry again. Both responded, "It's because you're bitter." It is remarkable that anybody would think that because a woman does not want to remarry that she is bitter. I let both of them know, with confidence that that was not the case. I was indisputably certain of that. If you have been accused of being bitter, investigate the validity; do some self-evaluation. If you find that bitterness has taken up residency, confess it to God. Seek counseling if you need help getting to the root and processing it. Confront whatever needs to be addressed. I've seen the word *bitterness* reframed as "hoarding hurt." That's an interesting perspective, and it's so true. Think about that for a moment. It means that the hurt is being saved, stashed, and stockpiled. I urge you to let bitterness go—do not hoard hurt.

Any act of betrayal can leave the betrayed person worn, and low in self-confidence and self-esteem. However, always take into consideration what God has to say about you above any negative words. Don't condemn yourself and don't give up—be strong and encourage yourself when needed. My sister, you are an awesome wonder and you have great value. Hold your head high and walk confidently. Be encouraged!

17
Life After Divorce

*"The Lord will guide you continually,
And satisfy your soul in drought,
And strengthen your bones;
You shall be like a watered garden,
And like a spring of water, whose waters do not fail."*
Isaiah 58:11

I almost started by posing the question, "*Is* there life after divorce?" But of course there is—no need to ask. I totally get that initially there could be setbacks and a temporary identity crisis, especially if you were in a long-term marriage. Nevertheless, hold on, I assure you, there *is* life after divorce.

The day of my divorce hearing was a little nerve-wrecking. We still had to finish business with the mediator and then there was the hearing, in which I was representing myself. I was legally inept, but financially deficient. I could only afford myself.

I thought I would need time off to recover from the hearing and the entire ordeal, but I returned to work the next day. Many family members and close friends inquired about the outcome of the hearing, to which I wittingly responded—I lost 220 pounds in one day. That was one way to describe it. I anticipated being a basket case and was shocked and confused when I was not. Two people clarified for me that it was because I had undergone so much of the grieving process already. I expected "something" to manifest as time went on, however I did not experience much grieving on that day, or during that week or in the months following.

Yes, I missed Andrew at first. I have heard people say that they still love someone from a former relationship, but are not *in* love with that person. Some have said that they will always have feelings for or even hold a special place in their heart for a former love. Well, more power to them. I asked God to totally remove any feelings of love that I had for Andrew. Most of the love was gone by the time of our divorce anyway. I felt it was unhealthy to house any residue from a dysfunctional love. Besides, if I ever did allow anyone else in my heart, all of that space would have to be vacant for the occupancy of my new man.

Different phases of the process might bring on varying emotions. Don't be afraid to feel what you are feeling during and after your divorce. If you are happy, excited and relieved, then bask in the ambiance of it. If you are angry, upset and disappointed, let it come up so that it can come out. Suppressing negative emotions is not a good thing. Those feelings need to be processed and managed in a healthy manner.

Grief is often experienced due to loss of the marriage. While grieving what you have lost you might find yourself likewise grieving what you potentially may miss out on. There are five stages to the grief process—denial, bargaining, depression, anger, and acceptance. I want to focus on the last stage for a moment—acceptance. At some point, there must be a coming to terms with the new reality—that the divorce has occurred. Acceptance doesn't mean you're happy about the divorce. It means acknowledgement or recognition of the fact. In actuality, when facing the truth and finally accepting the end of your marriage it might feel like a ten-ton weight has lifted from your shoulders. Once you no longer carry that weight, it will be easier to move on to a better life. Grieve it and leave it! I don't want to just throw a cliché out there, however, simplifying the viewpoint also adds a sense of relief. Go through the process, and then let it go. Be careful not to get stuck in route for an unhealthy period of time. Author and Christian counselor,

Steve Arterburn suggests that the "grief process is a healing of your future." With your future in sight, press through the stages to acceptance. If you do not have a good support system to help you through the grieving process, seek one out through church ministries, professional counsel, good friends, or trusted family.

Over the years, my sister has been a great source of strength and encouragement. In one of her countless reassuring emails she offered these words—*Looks like it's winding down for you and it will be a past chapter in your life. Think toward the new chapters; those unread, but anticipated. What is before you is a new house, companionship, healthy and educated children, grandchildren etc. Sometimes, when I go through things, I don't know why I had to go thru it till later. That's when it makes sense to me.* Thank you for your inspiration, big sis! What makes sense to me now is that one of my new chapters consists of helping you get to yours. Also, to let you know that I made it through and beyond any doubt you can too.

Enjoy the new chapters of *your* life. The door is wide open for you to experience things you have always wanted to. You can have a rich fulfilling life even though it may not feel like it at first. Reach for it. If need be, get a new vision for your life. Don't focus on what is currently unavailable. Start by focusing on what you have, and move toward achieving your desires.

One thing I didn't have was a man. At one point I became upset, borderline angry that I didn't have a special someone. My own "honeybunch" who I could call with news, good or bad; and who I could attend events with and think about as I awoke, and say goodnight to (on the phone) before falling asleep. Then it occurred to me, in that healing season of my life I didn't need a man. If I had one, *he* might have become my god, because he would be the one that I leaned and depended on to fill the voids. I needed God, the Almighty, not a rebound guy.

In addition to not having a man, a divorce may cause you to experience other forms of lack—physically, mentally, emotionally, and spiritually. Sometimes when men get in adulterous situations, they leave their wife high and dry. Wherever you are deficient, whatever you are lacking, ask God for it. Sometimes we don't ask God for things then wonder why we don't have them. What you need is not likely to just appear. God will supply your needs according to His riches in glory, which are not limited to finances. His riches go far beyond nickels and dimes. Whatever you stand in need of, ask for it. If you need understanding or godly guidance—ask for it! If it is peace that you need, ask God to help you keep your mind stayed on Him, He will keep you in perfect peace. If you need shelter, food, clothing, employment, friends, whatever—ask. Receiving is in the asking. In addition to going to God, inquire around and conduct internet searches to locate available resources and use them too. A woman enduring divorce can shift from having everything to having nothing. If that is your circumstance, seek your necessities, be encouraged, don't quit, fight through, and know that you can rebuild.

Here are some suggestions to help you rebuild and bounce back from the devastation of divorce.

- ~ God first—Always and in everything remember to keep God first.
- ~ Be sure to have your *daily* personal devotion time (praying and studying the Bible). This regular appointment with God is imperative whether or not you are in a challenging situation.
- ~ Connect with another local church—If you cannot or will not go to your home church, attend another Bible teaching church regularly for your spiritual nourishment. Stay connected.
- ~ Be transformed by the renewing of your mind—Watch what goes in…and stays there.
- ~ Speak positive words over yourself and your situation—I will, I am, I can.
- ~ Don't give up.

- ~ Take one day at a time—Plan for tomorrow but live in today.
- ~ Exhale, think, explore, process, relax.
- ~ Determine what you want—Take inventory; make measured decisions.
- ~ Be careful not to make life-altering decisions when caught up in your emotions.
- ~ Make healthy food choices—Your health, good or bad, affects your whole life.
- ~ Be okay with your new place in life—Embrace it and celebrate it.
- ~ Be fruitful, not busy—Do what counts.
- ~ Ease on down the road of self-discovery—Take the time to rediscover you.
- ~ Simplify—Purge the things from your life that don't matter, and are not needed.
- ~ Let go of the pain and the past—That focus will cause you to be off-balance.
- ~ Choose your attitude—See the glass as half full.
- ~ Don't be bitter! Being a bitter person can cause fear among everyone in your path. It is difficult for bitterness to go undetected. It is something that seeps through the pores and can present in behavior such as unpleasantness, harshness, and nastiness.

One of the suggestions above recommends embracing your new place in life. When you embrace and do not resist, you are more open to learning and growing. To embrace and even enjoy your journey—where you are, where you are going and everything in-between—should not be optional. It signifies that you are not stuck but realizing, accepting and making the absolute best of your journey. Learn from the roadblocks, detours, the slippery roads, the do not enters, stop signs, wrong ways, U-turns, and no turns. Accept the journey for what it is, get all that you can get from it, and remember that you are not travelling alone; God is with you.

On a plane ride from Colorado to California, I sat next to a man wearing a small brown cowboy hat. It was decorated with a fairly plain white button with black lettering. This little button conveyed a simple yet powerful and inspiring message. It read, "Live a great story." Wow! That is not something to merely ponder. That is a goal to actively strive for. It is attainable. Living a great story is within our reach. While we cannot control everything that happens in our lives, we do have the ability to change negatives into positives. We don't need to fabricate a storyline, but we can surely orchestrate one. We do not have to "let the chips fall where they may." We can turn things around by giving the chips direction.

> While we cannot control everything that happens in our lives, we do have the ability to change negatives into positives.

What will it take for *you* to live a great story? First, let me back up and assure you that your story isn't over. Nope, it isn't. Divorce is not your end. So, at this interval in your life, what will it take for you to live a great story?! Pause and imagine! Really take the time to survey, then you can plan and implement. The greatness of your story has yet to be experienced. Since you still have life, you have the opportunity to make it great. So, your mission, if you choose to accept it, is to *live a great story*.

While in California, I rented a car and brought along my not so always reliable GPS, (Richard). One morning I left my son's place to venture off to LA for a studio tour. As I was trying to listen to Richard *and* follow printed website directions, I got a little turned around. I even thought, "You should pull over and figure it out." But no, I kept travelling on for a bit. Had I taken the time, I would have realized that I had been in the area where I wanted to be. All I needed to do was turn around and go back a few yards on to Route 5 North. So close, yet unaware. As you are travelling along in life, you may be where you should be, you may be way off-course, or you may unknowingly be in the vicinity of your desired destination. Do you need to slow down long enough to figure out the right direction for your life? If necessary, pull over and get your bearings. Prayerfully decide what the best route is, and take it.

If you are looking back, please don't waste good time. There is nothing you can do to change the past; it is now history. If God wanted us to be looking back all of the time, He would have made us with eyes in the back of our heads. However, He did give us the ability to turn our heads for a temporary look back—we can review and learn from mistakes but without getting stuck there. It is challenging to look back while walking forward; the risk of crashing into something is quite probable. Or even worse, we can become something that we shouldn't; something we were not meant to be. Remember Lot's wife? She is the woman that turned into a pillar of salt. Why? What was she guilty of? Looking back (Genesis 19:26)! Being future focused is in your best interest. Where you are headed is what it's all about.

While you are being future focused, keep your eyes open for tricks of the enemy. In particular the rebound guy (I'll call him Cleophas)—watch out for him. Cleophas can enter the picture at any time and from anywhere. When and if you get a new man, let it be God's timing and God's guy. Don't rush into a relationship for the sake of convincing yourself, and showing others that you can get someone too. That resembles child's play and is unsafe terrain.

Since we are on the subject of focus, it would actually help to place your focus on someone other than you and yours. When going through, it is easy to become self-absorbed and consumed with what is going on in your own world. Redirect your focus, be a blessing—the essence of that theme was echoed to me over and over *after* my situation—or maybe that's when I actually tuned in to it. I felt so convicted hearing that because during my situation, I was so "woe is me." Me, me, me. Who can you help? Someone needs you! Whether independently or jointly working with an organization—reach out to another. You are not turning a blind eye or a deaf ear to your situation but while praying, fasting, and seeking God for you, you can assist someone else. There is plenty of work out there to do.

We can learn so many lessons while going through our individual journeys. Some basics are faith, trusting God, developing a closer spiritual walk, and patience. I would like to challenge you to inquire of God what He is specifically conveying to you. Sometimes God's message goes beyond the basics. I urge you to ascertain what His customized lesson plan is for you.

Some of you may know, as I do, that if you do not see reminders of something the possibility is very strong that it will be forgotten. Out of sight, out of mind. While you are regrouping, it is so important that you make plans and write them down. Set specific goals and write them down. Set deadlines—I want to accomplish this by that date and write it down. It can be logged in a journal, book or on a calendar—paper or electronic (preferably paper so you can post in an observable place). It should be organized, visible, and reviewed daily or at least weekly. If it is put away, especially in the kitchen junk drawer, it will be soon forgotten. Vison boards are very popular these days, but I am proposing more of a simple list outlining your goals and targeted deadlines. Update and tweak as needed. I am a procrastinator and when I do that long enough in any given situation, I am bound to forget. The result is not good—tasks don't get done and goals are not accomplished. Unfortunately, forgetting has caused me to miss out on many things. Having your plans and deadlines written will help you remember, making it easier to achieve them. If you are a person that is naturally organized or one that rarely forgets—keep doing what works for you.

I started writing notes for this book when I was still married. Here it is over sixteen years later and I am just finishing up. What happened? I worked full-time, raised two children, went to graduate school, became a grandma, endured the rejections of a book proposal—life happened—but that is just an excuse. The bottom line is I did not set goals, write them down, and keep them before me so that I could remember them and oversee them. I lost sight; therefore, as life went on, the manuscript of this book got dustier and dustier on the back shelf. It is easy to lose sight when goals and deadlines are not at the forefront. Perhaps the messages in this book could have been a blessing to many struggling women over the last *decade*.

For some, the issue may have been you did not write a plan or you wrote a plan but there was no implementation. In the meantime, life is going by. Nothing is happening. Your vision can become stagnant while you are waiting for things to just happen to you and for you. Even if you have a plan and you have God's favor you still have to put some work into it. While browsing around in a store I saw this on a plaque, "Good things come to those who hustle." Wherever it is you want to go in life, get a plan together: write it down, keep it visible, and implement it. Implementation is key! Get your hustle on. Think beyond your wildest notions and go for it. The question of the day is—*how badly do you want it?* That will determine just how much hustle you put into it.

You *can* make great things happen in your new fabulous life. It might seem overwhelming at times, but you can handle it. There is so much to look forward to. Life is still going on—do not let it pass you *bye*.

18

Don't Hate the Player, Hate the Game

> "You have heard that it was said, 'You shall love your neighbor and hate your enemy.' But I say to you, love your enemies, bless those who curse you, do good to those who hate you, and pray for those who spitefully use you and persecute you, that you may be sons of your Father in heaven…"
> Matthew 5:43-45a

While growing up, my mother, a wise woman, gave me advice that so many moms in her day gave their child when they bore the brunt of an offense: "Don't hate the person, hate what they did." Sound familiar? It is loosely based on biblical principles which have been passed on for generations. The essence of that phrase has evolved into, "Don't hate the player, hate the game," which has become popular in our culture.

"Playing" and "getting played" is all about deception, betrayal, manipulation, and self-centeredness. There is a biblical person that, I believe, forfeited some of his own blessings because he was too busy hating the player and the game. It is the brother of the prodigal son. He did not like the fact that his brother was welcomed back into the family in grand style after taking his own inheritance, leaving home and wasting it on "the good life." However, if there is ever a biblical person that would personify this jargon at both ends of the spectrum, it is our brother Jacob: the player, and the played! He played people and in return, he got played.

Just watch!

Jacob, on a *self-centered* mission to look out for number one, *deceived* his brother Esau out of his birthright through *manipulation* (Genesis 25:29-34). To further his cause, he *betrayed* his father Isaac, receiving the blessing due to Esau (Genesis 27:18-20). Jacob thought that he had won the gold and was preparing for his victory stand on the center circle, but the game was not over. As Jacob's life continued, he was blind to the fact that he was a player caught up in the cycle, aka, "the game." In enters his Uncle Laban, who eventually plays the player.

Initially, I thought it was a family thing since Jacob and Laban were related. Then I realized it is a human thing. Many of us, at one time or another, have looked out only for ourselves, no matter what the cost. If by chance it was not you (be honest with yourself), surely you know of someone who did!

The story is told in Genesis 29:21-27 that Laban gave his firstborn daughter Leah as a wife to Jacob. This transaction took place after Jacob worked for seven years for Laban's younger daughter, Rachel, his true love. It was a game of deception. You might recognize it as the ol' "bait and switch." Laban was setting the record straight in verse 26, "It must not be done so in our country, to give the younger before the firstborn." In other words, he was saying, I don't know how you do it in your country, but over here, this is how we roll. We don't marry off the younger daughter first.

Jacob was familiar with the game of deception; why would he succumb to its trickery? Could it be that Jacob "allowed" himself to get played because he wanted something—Rachel—so badly? It makes me wonder, did I allow myself to get played because I wanted something—successful marriage and ministry—so badly? What was in me—or lacking in me for that matter—that I would give license to such a travesty? When the realization of allowing myself to get played came, and self-assessing questions started overflowing my mind, it hit me like a ton of bricks. At that precise point, I didn't just hate the player; I hated me too! I cried for days.

When I say that I got played, I mean, I let Andrew call the shots; I just let things happen.

Hate is described by *Merriam-Webster.com* as "intense hostility and aversion usually deriving from fear, anger, or sense of injury." Hate is ugly. However, all things considered, it is hard not to hate the player…it is *so* hard not to hate the player! It is so *very* hard not to hate the player. Are you feeling me? I can remember times when it was simply unbearable to watch my husband stand up in the pulpit and proclaim the Word of God. I learned early to worship with a poker face. You know, the face that hides what's happening, as it is forbidden to reveal the hand. Remember the image: we, the pastor's family, are the "happy, perfect, godly" family.

Who did I see when I looked at Andrew? Did I see the man that hurt me, *or* the man that God desired to use? Oddly, I saw both, so I prayed for both. The only way that I found that I could transcend hating the player, was to try to see what God saw.

Okay, you caught me. Maybe there was a time that, because of my hurt, I didn't care what happened to Andrew. Eventually I concluded that the enemy was at work through the game.

We can formulate mega lists on why we *should* hate the player, but let's not go there. We have all experienced pain that we do not want to revisit. So, let's check out a few legitimate reasons why we *should not* hate the player.

- ~ The player has purpose, so try to see him from God's vantage point. Know that God is not finished with him; know that he can still be transformed into the man that God called and purposed him to be.
- ~ Hate hinders *your* blessings!!!
- ~ Your health is important! Hate can cause health related problems. Take good care of yourself, being careful not to allow hate to destroy you.

- Pay back's a… "V"—We don't need to worry about the player anyway because the Lord says, "Vengeance is Mine, I will repay" (Romans 12:19). God's gonna get him. Oops! Strike that from the record. How'd that get in there?
- "If someone says, "I love God," and hates his brother, he is a liar; for he who does not love his brother whom he has seen, how can he love God whom he has not seen" (I John 4:20)?
- "Hatred stirs up strife…" (Proverbs 10:12a).
- "But I say to you who hear: Love your enemies, do good to those who hate you, bless those who curse you, and pray for those who spitefully use you" (Luke 6:27-28).
- God orchestrates events for the ultimate good. "But as for you, you meant evil against me; *but* God meant it for good, in order to bring it about as *it is* this day, to save many people alive. Now therefore, do not be afraid…" (Genesis 50:20-21a).

Jeremiah 29:11 is Andrew's favorite Bible verse. This verse is also chief among favorites for many people. However, if a person is going to lay claim to verse 11, verses 12-14 should be included.

> *For I know the thoughts that I think toward you, says the Lord, thoughts of peace and not of evil, to give you a future and a hope. Then you will call upon Me and go and pray to Me, and I will listen to you. And you will seek Me and find Me, when you search for Me with all your heart. I will be found by you, says the Lord, and I will bring you back from your captivity; I will gather you from all the nations and from all the places where I have driven you, says the Lord, and I will bring you to the place from which I cause you to be carried away captive.*

God will fulfill his purpose in the one who is searching for Him with their entire heart. It may not be evident right away when a wayward soul starts seeking God again. We never know when, where or how God is going to move on someone's heart, bringing that individual back to Him. God can still bring His special plans to pass in the life of a repented person. Perhaps Jeremiah 29:11 is an undeclared favorite, yet applicable Scripture for your husband as well.

I believe that God is always doing more than just one thing at a time. He can enclose many purposes in any given situation. We are sometimes guilty of limiting Him based on our incomplete insight. Unfortunately, the easiest response to have in the circumstances that you are facing may be hatred toward your spouse; however, be careful not to allow hate to rule you. Even though indicators may make it seem like a game, look for something good to come out of it. God knows what He is doing, all of the time. When it comes down to it, don't hate the player or the game because God knows the plans that He has for your husband. They are plans to give him a future and a hope.

19
We're All Human

*"Blessed is the man who endures temptation;
for when he has been approved,
he will receive the crown of life which the Lord has
promised to those who love Him."*
James 1:12

I'm human, you're human—*we're all human*. We are subject to errors in judgment and all kinds of fleshly infractions, commonly known as sin. We're guilty of doing things that God told us not to do and not doing the things that He told us to do. They are sins of *commission*—doing what we should not do, and sins of *omission*—don't do what we should. The presence of evil surrounds us despite our aspirations to do good (Romans 7:21).

Regardless of our good intentions, God's expectation is that we live according to His standard of holiness, and not man's interpretation of it. He wants us to be holy in our conduct, as reflected in I Peter 1:15-16, "But as He who called you *is* holy, you also be holy in all your conduct, because it is written, 'Be holy, for I am holy.'" That command conflicts with human nature. Although my heart wants to do what pleases God, my flesh wants to do what pleases me. That can cause a mini war within my being; and it has. The struggle is real, yet we are required to live holy. And we can, because God is not going to tell us to do something that He has not equipped us to do. "Holy" is not a word used much or a lifestyle pursued by humans in general. Nonetheless, God has not weakened His stance on holiness.

Dealing with the fallout from infidelity can propel you into a vulnerable position, so be cognizant of your state of mind. If a person that has been hurt, or is hurting, is not watchful, the same sin that ensnared their spouse—or something worse—can become a downfall for them too. I can imagine that some "abandoned" wives have responded to their pain by willfully entering into an illicit relationship; an entanglement, if you will. It is not worth paying the price. The pleasure of sin for a moment can yield a lifetime of regret. Grace was not afforded to us so that we could haphazardly sin out of our pain. Attempting to satisfy needs or wants can ruin two homes. Just because a person violated their marital covenant doesn't give license to the other spouse to do so as well. Walk in wisdom, being conscious not to allow your situation to cloud good judgment and decision-making. Be encouraged and determined to stay on the straight and narrow. You will thank yourself and do a happy dance later.

Payback by having an affair might seem justified, but that is not the answer. "There is a way *that seems* right to a man, but its end *is* the way of death" (Proverbs 16:25). Some go into sinful situations deceptively thinking they can handle the consequences only to find the result is more than bargained for. Cocky confidence is a lure of the enemy. Besides for adultery being a sin, the tit-for-tat mentality is a big web to weave. One sin begets another. There are numerous lies and dreadful cover-ups. The entire situation could blow up into a senseless soap opera drama.

I understand the yearning to be desired. I totally get it. I craved compliments and attention. After being rejected, verbally and emotionally, I needed the affirmation. A year or so after we separated, I really wanted to start dating. I began to rationalize (to make "rational lies") in my mind that Andrew already divorced me emotionally. At that juncture, I was in a danger zone. Emotional divorce is not legal divorce—there is no Scripture reference to support that thinking. As long as a husband and wife are still legally married, paperwork and all—they are still married. Be careful not to allow the enemy to trick you in that regard.

I began this chapter acknowledging that we are human. However, being human is not an excuse to sin. It's a reason, but not an excuse, especially when God has given us the power through His Holy Spirit to overcome temptations. Sometimes the opportunity to sin shows up "spur-of-the-moment," it's spontaneous. Then there are times when it is calculated and carefully planned out. We actually make plans to transgress. Insert raised hand emoji here, because *I* have made plans to sin. Have you? Think about this—within the time it takes to rationalize and figure out and justify wrong, that is plenty enough time to back out and say, "I can't do this; I won't do this." While it is true that God is faithful and just to forgive and cleanse us upon confession of our sins (I John 1: 9), that is not justification to live a slackened life.

The next time and every time you and I plan to sin, we must think about, in addition to the severe consequences, how it affects God. Will it be said of you, "but the thing that (your name) had done displeased the Lord?" That's what was said of David (II Samuel 11:27). We *must* factor in the cost. Displeasing God is major. Additionally, without holiness (sanctification) no man shall see God. Hebrews 12:14 says, "Pursue peace with all people, and holiness, without which no one will see the Lord." I believe that doesn't just mean not "seeing" the Lord in heaven. Sin disrupts our rapport with God. The disconnect induced by sin affects our relationship *now*. When we aren't living right, we miss experiencing God—seeing Him—to the fullest. We are in the position to receive God's blessings when we continue to live a righteous and holy life. God rewards obedience. Determine to keep your eyes on the finish line. Strive to live a holy life deliberately.

There is nothing new under the sun. The temptations you are confronted with have been encountered down through the ages. Scripture lets us know that, "No temptation has overtaken you except such as is common to man; but God *is* faithful, who will not allow you to be tempted beyond what you are able, but with the temptation will also make the way of escape, that you may be able to bear it" (I Corinthians 10:13). When approached by temptation to sin, look for the escape hatch. Even if it is "just" recalling Scripture, and remembering that there are consequences attached to actions. If you don't see the escape, ask God where it is, because it's within reach. Also, know that God's grace is a balance for the temptation you face. His grace is sufficient (II Corinthians 12:9) and is available in your time of need.

> *Calling sin by its name and realizing that involvement in it will only result in a downward spiral may lessen the possibility of willing participation.*

Calling sin by its name and realizing that involvement in it will only result in a downward spiral may lessen the possibility of willing participation. Moreover, the temptation will be kept alive by feeding it with constant thoughts of partaking in it. Don't even entertain thoughts of sin. Furthermore, it's easier to say "*no*" before embroiled in sin than saying "*no*" in the middle of it. Especially with sex; once the ball gets rolling, it can be hard to stop. It's best not to even get started.

We don't know when temptation will come but be ready because the truth of the matter is, it's coming in some way, shape, or form. Think in advance about the magnitude of your choices—the effect it will have on you and your loved ones, maybe even for generations to come. Be real with yourself. Know your limitations and stay far away from the danger zone. Have a strategic plan ready. Below are some elements to include.

- ~ Prepare with pre-prayer! Even if you *think* you won't have an issue with temptation—pray about it anyway.
- ~ Don't concoct "rational lies." The truth will make you free. Stick with what is true.
- ~ Keep a list handy of "consequence" Scriptures such as, "For the wages of sin is death" (Romans 6:23). Review them when tempted.

- ~ Keep a list handy of "comfort" Scriptures. You may be more vulnerable to temptation when feeling sorry for yourself. Locate and memorize Bible verses that minister to your hurt. Read Isaiah 41:10, John 14:27, and Romans 8:28.
- ~ Have a "bottom line" Scripture. That is the specific Bible verse that will help keep you in check. My bottom line Scripture was Proverbs 31:28a. (This may surprise you.)
- ~ Have a standby prayer partner—*she* doesn't have to be a daily partner, but someone you can count on, can trust, and will pray with and for you.
- ~ Look at your face in the mirror. Can you live with your decisions? Will you be able to look at yourself after you willingly participate in sin? That's the same face you will have to continue to look at every day—you can't hide from you.
- ~ Repeat to yourself morning, noon, and night, "I will hold firm to my integrity."

I went through a season of temptation a while after the start of Andrew's affair. As I was facing temptation, I knew that my hope was in the Word of God. So, I had to cling to it. Yet it was not just Scriptures like, "His grace is sufficient," that aided me. It was this unsuspecting verse, that helped to keep my focus, "Her children rise up and call her blessed" (Proverbs 31:28a). That was my bottom line Scripture. I wanted my children to one day speak well of me and call *me* blessed. In addition to loving me, I wanted them to respect and honor me too. It matters what my children think of me. Succumbing to temptation could have jeopardized that likelihood.

I can't emphasize this enough—know yourself and know your limitations and weaknesses. However, don't hoodwink yourself by being overconfident. "Therefore let him who thinks he stands take heed lest he fall" (I Corinthians 10:12). Watch and evaluate your decisions. If you are not sure about them, or if you find yourself on the verge of doing something you shouldn't—reach out—to God, Scriptures, friends, your support team. As discussed, you don't have to go through this alone. However, be careful of who you allow to influence you. Don't get it twisted: "Evil company corrupts good habits" (I Corinthians 15:33). Who do you hang out with? It would not be surprising if old friends, male or female, start showing up. The enemy knows how to throw in diversions. This brings me back to the rebound guy, Cleophas. I mentioned him in an earlier chapter. The interesting thing is, Cleophas may not be packaged in your preferred taste. He may be the complete opposite, but, saying just what you need to hear and doing just what you need done. He's real. Keep your eyes open.

Endeavoring to become closer to one another when dating, Andrew and I decided to share what we considered our deepest secret. A day and time was planned for the big reveal. We promised each other to keep the secrets between us. What Andrew told me has and will always remain a secret, unless *he* chooses to make it known. What I told him, I also told a couple of other people and now will share with you.

When I went away to college, I met the proverbial tall, dark, and handsome man, not to mention athletic too. We became friends immediately. One thing that he disclosed to me early on was that he was married, but separated. So unfortunately, I had to keep him at a distance. This was pre-cell phone era so it was a little easier. We did talk on the phone, occasionally visited each other, and once or twice went out. The downside of doing those things is that you can start to develop feelings, as we did. Against my better judgement, I allowed him to kiss me. While we never had sex nor was ever close to it, the kiss was wrong. We live in a culture today where that behavior is acceptable, even to become engaged to other people while married to someone else. We hear about these situations amongst famous people from time to time, and not much is thought of it. Nevertheless, until two people are divorced they are *still* married and that covenant should *still* be honored. That is God's way and that is what matters.

At points while writing the manuscript I felt weird, considering what I just disclosed. However, as you can attest from reading this book, I don't bash Andrew for what he did. The book is not about condemning him. That was never my goal. Nor was my endeavor to portray myself as haughty, I fall short too. My main objective is to share strategies on how to survive the various occurrences that arise because of infidelity. *We're all human.*

20

And Finally My Sister

> "The Lord bless you and keep you; the Lord
> make his face shine upon you and be gracious
> to you; The Lord lift up His countenance
> upon you, and give you peace."
>
> Numbers 6:24-26

You know what's funny? Not "ha, ha, chuckle, chuckle" funny, but "interesting" funny. Years ago, when the Lord birthed this book in my bosom, I really did not have much to write. The scenario would have been simple—my husband had an affair, he stopped, I forgave him, and we skipped off into a beautifully colored sunset. Instead, I experienced considerably more than I ever imagined possible. I would not go so far as to send Andrew's mistress a box of chocolates and a thank you card, but I rest in the fact that what happened has purpose.

I believe that God allowed more "adventure," if you will, in my story, so that in the long run, I would be a learning tool, a voice, and a source of guidance and inspiration for others. My hardships and trials were not endured in vain. I'm able to share my experience and am happy to do so in the assurance that what I'm passing on to you will help and comfort you. Therefore, what I survived was not just for me; it was for you too. Please learn from my mistakes, my earned knowledge, and my God-inspired insight. I became transparent so that you could see clearly, and I have comforted you with that which the Lord has comforted me.

It is my prayer that the effects of your circumstances don't leave you scarred, and that there will be no residue on any aspect of your being. And, that you won't look like what you have been through. People will only know your story because you told them, not because they can see it on you.

Take courage, you are doing great—keep on going—you are awesome—you are going to make it. Be strong, be confident, be positive, be refreshed, be blessed! With God's help, you can and you will survive the ultimate betrayal!

Finally, my sister, "*be strong in the Lord* and in the power of *His* might" (Ephesians 6:10).

> *Now to Him who is able to keep you from stumbling,*
> *And to present you faultless before the presence of*
> *His glory with exceeding joy, to God our Savior,*
> *Who alone is wise, be glory and majesty, dominion*
> *and power, both now and forever. Amen.*
>
> Jude 24-25

A Special Gift

As you know, *Surviving the Ultimate Betrayal* is a book about betrayal in the marital relationship. However, the ultimate betrayal of all time is sin. God loves you! He has a wonderful, tailor-made plan for your life and desires a relationship with you. However, sin is a barrier to that relationship. The Bible says, "all have sinned and fall short of the glory of God" (Romans 3:23). Sin is "wrongdoing"; it's "a missing of the mark" by not living according to God's laws/standards/principles. The penalty for sin is death—separation from God (Romans 6:23a).

Thankfully, God loves us so much that He remedied the situation—"the gift of God is eternal life in Christ Jesus our Lord" (Romans 6:23b). He sent His son, Jesus, to pay the price for sin, provide us with the means to live a fulfilled life, and a promise to be with Him for eternity. Romans 10:9-10 & 13 declares, "if you confess with your mouth the Lord Jesus and believe in your heart that God has raised Him from the dead, you will be saved. For with the heart one believes unto righteousness, and with the mouth confession is made unto salvation. … 'whoever calls on the name of the Lord shall be saved.'"

God loves you and will not betray you. When all is said and done, it's your relationship with *Him* that matters most.

If you have not made that very crucial decision to have a relationship with God (which starts by accepting Jesus as your Savior) you can do so *right now*. It is as easy as A, B, C:

A—Admit that you are a sinner and repent, which is to turn from your sins

B—Believe in your heart that Jesus died (for your sins) and that God raised Him from the dead

C—Confess that Jesus is Lord

If you agree with those things and want to accept Jesus as your Savior, simply pray this prayer.

Dear God, I admit that I am a sinner. I believe in my heart that your Son Jesus died for my sins and that you raised Him from the dead. Please forgive me for my sins, I am truly sorry and now turn away from my sins and turn to you. Help me to live according to your Word. I confess that Jesus is Lord and I invite Him to take control and to become the Lord of my life, from this day forward. Thank you for loving me, for forgiving me, and for saving me. In Jesus' name. Amen.

If you prayed that prayer and believed it in your heart, then God has saved you through your faith in Christ Jesus! Welcome to the family of God!

Here are some great next steps: (1) Spend time with God every day through prayer and studying the Bible; (2) Join a local Bible teaching church where you can worship God, grow spiritually, and fellowship with other believers; (3) Get baptized (an outward expression of an inside change).

Notes

Chapter One – *Call It What It Is*
1. Infidelity. (2017). In *Merriam-Webster.com*. Retrieved from https://www.merriam-webster.com/dictionary/infidelity
2. Infidelity. (2017). In *Dictionary.com*. Retrieved from http://www.dictionary.com/browse/infidelity
3. New Life Live! [Radio program]. Lake Forest, CA.
4. Familiar. (2017). In *Merriam-Webster.com*. Retrieved from https://www.merriam-webster.com/dictionary/familiar

Chapter Three – *Where I Went Wrong*
New Life Live! [Radio program]. Lake Forest, CA.

Chapter Four – *What God Has Joined Together*
1. Covenant. (2017). In *Merriam-Webster.com*. Retrieved from https://www.merriam-webster.com/dictionary/covenant?src=search-dict-hed
2. Covenant. (2017). *Baker's Evangelical Dictionary of Biblical Theology*. Retrieved from http://www.biblestudytools.com/dictionary/covenant/

Chapter Five – *Moving Forward*
Joyce Meyer referenced quotes are verbal quotes taken from her sermons viewed on YouTube videos and television broadcasts.

Chapter Six – *Too Legit to Quit*
1. Hammer, MC. (1991). Too legit to quit [Recorded by MC Hammer]. On *Too legit to quit* [Vinyl record]. Hollywood, CA: Capitol Records.
2. Quit. (2017). In *Dictionary.com*. Retrieved from http://www.dictionary.com/browse/quit
3. Wallis, E. (1987). *Queen take your throne*. Cityhill Pub
4. Good. (2017). In *Dictionary.com*. Retrieved from http://www.dictionary.com/browse/good

Chapter Seven – *Pray Without Ceasing*
Barnes' notes on the Bible. (2017). In *Biblehub.com*. Retrieved from http://biblehub.com/commentaries/hebrews/4-16.htm

Notes

Chapter Eight – *Support Team*
Joyce Meyer referenced quotes are verbal quotes taken from her sermons viewed on YouTube videos and television broadcasts.

Chapter Nine – *The Other Woman*
1. Kidney, R. & McLaughlin, C. (Producer), & Luketic, R. (Director). (2001). *Legally Blonde* [Motion picture]. United States: Metro-Goldwyn-Mayer Studios.
2. New Life Live! [Radio program]. Lake Forest, CA.
3. Holcomb, Justin S., (2013). *On the grace of god*. Wheaton, Illinois: Crossway.

Chapter Ten – *Freedom to Forgive*
Cannon, R. (Producer), & Grant, D. (Director). (2005). *Diary of a Mad Black Woman* [Film]. United States: The Tyler Perry Company

Chapter Eleven – *Surviving*
1. Surviving. (2017). In *Dictionary.com*. Retrieved from http://www.dictionary.com/browse/surviving
2. Tkaczyk, F. (2016). *Six basic survival skills*. Retrieved from https://www.wildernesscollege.com/basic-survival-skills.html.
3. Lewis, R.M. (2017). History. In *KeepCalmandCarryOn.com*. Retrieved from http://www.keepcalmandcarryon.com/history/
4. Poker face. (2017). In *Merriam-Webster.com*. Retrieved from https://www.merriam-webster.com/dictionary/poker%20face

Chapter Twelve – *By Faith*
Faith. (2018). In *Merriam-Webster.com*. Retrieved from https://www.merriam-webster.com/dictionary/faith

Chapter Thirteen – *Fear*
1. Rebuke. (2020). In *Biblehub.com*. Retrieved from https://biblehub.com/topical/r/rebuke.htm
2. Joyce Meyer referenced quotes are verbal quotes taken from her sermons viewed on YouTube videos and television broadcasts.

Chapter Fourteen – *The Children*
New Life Live! [Radio program]. Lake Forest, CA.

Chapter Fifteen – *Legally Speaking*
Guillen, L. (n.d.). *Emergency temporary child custody*. Retrieved from https://www.lawyers.com/legal-info/family-law/child-custody/emergency-temporary-child-custody.html

Chapter Sixteen – *A Word of Encouragement*
Joy. (2018) In *Dictionary.com*. Retrieved from http://www.dictionary.com/browse/joy

Chapter Seventeen – *Life After Divorce*
New Life Live! [Radio program]. Lake Forest, CA.

Chapter Eighteen – *Don't Hate the Player, Hate the Game*
Hate. (2017). In *Merriam-Webster.com*. Retrieved from https://www.merriam-webster.com/dictionary/hate?src=search-dict-hed

A Special Gift
Sin. Taken from *The new strong's expanded exhaustive concordance of the bible* by Strong, James. Copyright © 2010 by Thomas Nelson Publishers. Used by permission of Thomas Nelson. www.thomasnelson.com

About the Author

Patricia A. Tucker formerly served as director of women's ministries and facilitator of small groups. She serves on various ministries at the church she attends, First Baptist Church of Glenarden, including as a contributing writer for the women's ministry publication, *Grace Magazine*. For more than 20 years, Patricia has been an active member of Clergymates of Prince Georges County, a support group for pastor's wives.

She has earned a Bachelor of Science in psychology and a Master of Science in management. Patricia has several book manuscripts in progress. *Surviving the Ultimate Betrayal: A Woman's Guide to Navigating the Fallout from Infidelity* is her first published book.

Thank you for reading *Surviving the Ultimate Betrayal!*

Hugs,
Pat

www.ingramcontent.com/pod-product-compliance
Lightning Source LLC
Chambersburg PA
CBHW030813090426
42736CB00027B/496